With the acceptance into service of the Panzerkampfwagen V Panther in mid-1943, Oberkommando des Heeres, the high command of the army, ordered that each of the Panzer divisions should receive a battalion of the new tanks. As the Panthers were still undergoing trials in Germany at this time it was anticipated that units would receive their allocation at training facilities in Germany as the vehicles left the assembly lines. On 24 September 1943, following the tank's baptism of fire in Operation Citadel, a further directive clarified the proposed reorganisation by ordering that each Panzer regiment's I.Abteilung would be equipped with Panthers organised into four companies each and the battalions would be rotated to Germany as they could be spared from the front (1).

By late December 1943, as increasing numbers of tanks left the assembly lines, battalions from Panzer-Regiment 1, Panzer-Regiment 2, Panzer-Regiment 23, Panzer-Regiment 31, SS-Panzer-Regiment 1 and SS-Panzer-Regiment 2 had been converted to Panthers and returned to the front. Many other units were in training or heading to Germany and a total of 1,495 Panthers had been shipped to operational and instructional units by the end of the year (2).

One of the battalions in training during late 1943 was III.Abteilung of Panzer-Regiment 4 which had been detached from 13.Panzer-Division and transferred, at first to Austria, and eventually to Mailly-le-Camp in France where the crews received their new tanks. It had always been the intention to return the battalion to its parent formation, which spent the latter part of 1943 fighting around Krivoy Rog, modern-day Kryvyi Rih in central Ukraine, but in the event this would be the only Panther battalion to take part in the Italian campaign.

After a swift victory in Sicily, the Allies had lost no time in crossing to the Italian mainland but the subsequent advances had been meagre and painfully slow. The fighting in southern Italy also occurred at a time when Hitler was consumed by the defensive battles taking place on the Eastern Front. But with the creation of a bridgehead on the Anzio beaches, just 30 kilometres from the outer suburbs of Rome, in late January 1944, it was decided that a strong armoured force would be needed to eliminate the Allied foothold and within days of receiving its last shipment of tanks I.Abteilung, Panzer-Regiment 4, as it had been renamed, was ordered to the Italian Front.

With the exception of the Tiger, the Pzkpfw V Panther is probably the best known German armoured fighting vehicle of the Second World War period. But the tank enjoyed mixed success in Italy. On the open plains of the Ukraine and eastern Poland these vehicles performed spectacularly, destroying Soviet tanks at ranges of up to 2,000 metres. But in the rugged terrain of Italy, where the horizon was often just a few hundred metres away, the advantages conferred by their 7.5cm guns were greatly reduced. Forced to operate with few if any recovery facilities, the mechanically fragile Panthers suffered acordingly and more were lost to mechanical failure than enemy action. Added to this the tanks were rarely employed in battalion, or even company, sized operations.

1. Some regiments allocated the Panthers to their II.Abteilung. The tank's early history and initial unit establishments are discussed in detail in *TankCraft 34: Panther Medium Tank German Army and Waffen SS, Eastern Front Summer, 1943.*

2. This figure of course includes replacements but is impressive nonetheless.

A Panther ausf A of I.Abteilung, Panzer-Regiment 4 photographed near Monte Cassino in April or May 1944. The grid worked into the Zimmerit coating would suggest that this vehicle was assembled by Daimler-Benz. Other images in this series show that this tank was fitted with the so-called letterbox machine-gun aperture.

The main map shows Italy north of Salerno, which was the site of the joint British and American assault of 9 September 1943. The successive defensive lines, beginning with the Volturno Line north of Naples, are shown as broken lines and in most cases they are referred to by their anglicised names. Note that the Gothic Line, the scene of some of the bitterest fighting of the campaign, is actually made up of two distinct defensive lines named Green I and Green II. The smaller map at left shows the area south of Salerno and the Calabrian coast where the British and Canadian landings took place from 3 September 1943 at Reggio Calabria. In northern Italy the Operationszone Adriatisches Küstenland (OZAK) and Operationszone Alpenvorland (OZAV) were German military zones set up after the Italian surrender. The Italian Social Republic (RSI) was created on 23 September 1943 with Mussolini at its head and was nominally in control of the area north of Cassino. Its troops, however, fought under German command and from late November 1943 the defence of Italy was coordinated by the commander of Heeresgruppe C under the newly-created Oberbefehlshaber Südwest with Generalfeldmarschall Kesselring filling both roles.

On 3 September 1943, after securing Sicily, the Allies crossed the Straits of Messina and landed at Reggio Calabria on the Italian mainland. German units stationed in Italy at that time were technically under the orders of the Commando Supremo, the Italian high command, but any pretence of cooperation was dropped when the Italian government announced its surrender less than a week later and the Germans quickly moved to disarm their former allies. The main purpose of the landings along the Calabrian coast had been to distract the attention of the German commanders while another landing took place further north at Salerno. But the defenders were not to be so easily deceived and Generalfeldmarschall Albert Kesselring, who had been appointed to command all German military units in the Mediterranean, held back LXXVI.Panzerkorps, his powerful mobile reserve, correctly predicting that the main Allied effort would come at either Salerno or Naples. While the units in Calabria battled their way north and the formations at Salerno attempted to enlarge their bridgehead, the Germans methodically and calmly fell back on a succession of defensive positions, destroying the roads and bridges behind them. By the end of 1943 the Allied armies had reached positions about 100 kilometres south of Rome but now faced the fortifications of the Gustav Line, which the Germans had been reinforcing for months, in addition to tank and assault gun battalions which were making their way towards the front. The most important events of the campaign, particularly as they relate to the Panzer units, are set out below.

3 January 1944. The British begin their attacks against the Gustav Line. On the following day, the Americans assault the German positions on the Bernhardt Line.

12 January 1944. In appalling weather, the Americans begin their assault on the Gustav Line, capturing the town of Cervaro on the Rapido River.

15 January 1944. XIV.Panzerkorps abandons Monte Trocchio, south of Cassino, and withdraws across the Rapido River.

21 January 1944. The tanks of 15.Panzergrenadier-Division succeed in eliminating the American bridgeheads along the Rapido River. Later that day the Germans are reinforced by 29.Panzergrenadier-Division and 90.Panzergrenadier-Division. Under the cover of darkness the Americans cross the river and establish several small footholds but they are all wiped out on the following day.

22 January 1944. Allied troops land at Anzio against almost no opposition.

24 January 1944. As the Allies batter away at the Gustav Line Hitler orders that the German defensive positions are to be held at all costs. In Germany the first elements of I.Abteilung, Panzer-Regiment 4 leave for the Italian Front.

28 January 1944. The Germans mount the first counterattack against the Allied beachhead at Anzio.

30 January 1944. Allied forces attack from the Anzio beachhead toward Cisterna and Campoleone. None of the objectives are achieved and an entire American battalion is lost.

1 February 1944. German units along the Rapido River fall back toward Monte Cassino.

2 February 1944. A further attempt to take Cisterna fails while on the following day an American attempt to break out of the Anzio beachhead runs head-on into a German counterattack.

4 February 1944. A German attack at Anzio penetrates the Allied defences bringing the supply dumps on the beach under fire before being beaten back.

Photographed near Anzio in mid-February 1944 this tank is one of three Panzerbefehlswagen V command vehicles that were on hand with I.Abteilung, Panzer-Regiment 4 at the time. Note the rack with its antenna extensions under the tube for the gun cleaning rods on the hull side. Although difficult to see here, the armoured plug fitted to the machine-gun aperture in the main gun mantlet is just visible over the radio operator's left shoulder. These modifications were identifying features of these purpose-built vehicles. The complete lack of Zimmerit and the presence of a number of 16-bolt road wheels suggest that this tank was assembled prior to August 1943 although it has been retro-fitted with the TZF.12a monocular gun sight.

During the first days of February 1944 the tanks of I.Abteilung, Panzer-Regiment 4 reached Rome after completing the last 130 kilometres of the trip on their own tracks. A number were photographed during the parade of US Army prisoners that took place in the city at that time and this early production Panther ausf A from the battalion's 2.Kompanie is probably one of those. This vehicle is also shown and discussed on page 17 of the Camouflage & Markings section of this book.

5 February 1944. US Army units reach the outskirts of Cassino but fail to take the town.

7 February 1944. After two days of exchanging artillery fire the Germans launch a night attack on the Anzio beachhead.

8 February 1944. US troops conduct a major assault toward Monte Cassino while the Germans retake Aprilia, north of Anzio.

11 February 1944. An attack from the Anzio beachhead is repulsed by the Germans who have been intercepting Allied radio messages for days. On the previous day the German forces around Anzio had been reinforced by 4.Fallschirmjäger-Division. A further attack towards Monte Cassino is beaten back.

15 February 1944. Throughout the day Allied bombers and artillery pound the Benedictine monastery on Monte Cassino. An attempt to capture a nearby German position fails.

16 February 1944. The Germans launch a major offensive codenamed Operation Fischfang against the Allied beachhead at Anzio. More than seven divisions are thrown at the enemy positions including 3.Panzergrenadier-Division and 26.Panzer-Division. The Panthers of Panzer-Regiment 4 go into action for the first time north-west of Aprilia.

20 February 1944. Operation Fischfang comes to an end. Although initially successful, the Germans are defeated by a combination of the weather and Allied firepower.

29 February 1944. A third German offensive is launched at the Anzio beachhead but fails to dislodge the Allied troops.

1 March 1944. Panzer-Regiment 4 reports that just thirty Panther tanks, from an authorised strength of seventy-six, are fully operational. Most of the losses are due to mechanical failures.

15 March 1944. After a lengthy bombardment the third major Allied attempt to take Monte Cassino begins. Although a number of peripheral positions fall to the Allies, the defenders in the monastery hold out.

18 March 1944. An attack by New Zealand troops at Cassino ends with the loss of an entire tank company.

24 March 1944. At Anzio the Allied positions are subjected to heavy artillery bombardments and attacks by guided bombs. The German defenders along the Gustav Line continue to hold out.

April 1944. With both sides exhausted a period referred to as the 'big war of little battles' begins. In scenes reminiscent of the First World War, artillery duels and trench raids become the order of the day.

10 May 1944. Panzer-Regiment 4 reports that less than ten tanks are available for operations. On the following day the Allies launch Operation Diadem, the fourth and final attempt to take Cassino.

12 May 1944. Although the Allies are able to establish a bridgehead across the Rapido River and reinforce it with tanks, the paratroopers of 1.Fallschirmjäger-Division hold on in the ruins of the monastery.

13 May 1944. Allied troops capture Sant'Angelo and Castelforte outflanking the German defences in the Liri valley.

17 May 1944. German troops begin the evacuation of Monte Cassino and a general withdrawal from the Gustav Line. On the following day the ruins of the Monte Cassino monastery are secured by Polish troops.

20 May 1944. The Americans take the town of Gaeta on the coast south of Rome.

23 May 1944. Three American and two British divisions launch an assault from the Anzio beachhead which ends in stalemate. In a series of skirmishes between Pontecorvo and Ceprano the Panthers of 4.Kompanie, Panzer-Regiment 4 claim the destruction of thirty-three Allied tanks. The company commander, Hauptmann Josef Eck in Panther 401, personally accounts for three Sherman tanks and is later awarded the Ritterkreuz for his actions.

25 May 1944. *Elements of Panzer-Division Herman Göring defend Valmontone on the Caesar C Line, just 20 kilometres from the centre of Rome, against a strong armoured force. At high cost, the Americans take Cisterna while contact is made with the formations in the Anzio beachhead.*

26 May 1944. *The American tanks attacking Valmontone are ordered north toward Rome.*

30 May 1944. *The Americans force a gap between I.Fallschirmkorps and LXXXVI.Panzerkorps defending the Caesar C Line allowing a breakout from Anzio.*

2 June 1944. *Allied units overrun the German Caesar C Line south of Rome.*

4 June 1944. *US Army units enter Rome unopposed. The city's strategic value is negligible and any propaganda advantage is soon negated by the news that the Allies have landed in Normandy. Importantly Generaloberst von Vietinghoff's 10.Armee, including the Panzers of the Hermann Göring division and 15.Panzer-Grenadier-Division, is allowed to escape.*

6 June 1944. *During the next ten days, against little opposition, the Allies capture Tivoli, Civitavecchia on the coast, Civita Castellana and Orvieto and advance as far as Spoleto and Foligno, an important road junction on the Topino River at the foot of the Appenines.*

21 June 1944. *Advancing past Perugia, the British are held up at a line of outposts, most notably around the village of Sanfatucchio on the eastern side of Lake Trasimene.*

2 July 1944. *The Germans evacuate Siena.*

16 July 1944. *British troops capture Arezzo on the Trasimene Line and cross the Arno River. In the next few days the Germans abandon Livorno leaving behind over 25,000 booby traps.*

23 July 1944. *American troops enter Pisa.*

4 August 1944. *The Germans abandon Florence.*

25 August 1944. *The British launch Operation Olive, a major assault on the Gothic Line.*

28 August 1944. *2.Kompanie, Panzer-Regiment 4 claims the destruction of more than twelve enemy tanks in a single action near Cerasa, south of Fano.*

30 August 1944. *Canadian armoured units conduct the first attack on Pesaro but are beaten back after losing over thirty tanks.*

1 September 1944. *The commander of I.Abteilung, Panzer-Regiment 4 reports that 1.Kompanie and 3.Kompanie have no tanks. Within 48 hours Canadian troops penetrate the initial defences of the Gothic Line but fail to break through the so-called Green II positions behind the main front.*

4 September 1944. *As part of Operation Olive, British troops launch the first of eleven futile assaults on Gemmano, south-west of San Marino.*

12 September 1944. *In two days of savage fighting, Canadian and British armoured units capture Coriano, a major position on the Gothic Line.*

15 September 1944. *Indian units finally push the Grenadiers of 98.Infanterie-Division out of their positions around Gemmano.*

22 September 1944. *US Army troops capture the Il Giogo pass on the Gothic Line.*

26 September 1944. *The German defences along the Uso River north of Rimini, made up of paratroopers from Fallschirmjäger-Regiment 1 and an Ostlegion infantry battalion, are overwhelmed by British armoured units.*

The date given for this photograph of late summer is almost certainly correct but despite my best efforts I have been unable to establish a location. The original tank 401 was destroyed in late May 1944, and is shown on page 19 of the Camouflage & Markings section. The Kugelblende machine-gun mount suggests that this vehicle may be one of the replacements received in the following June but could just as likely have come from one of the other companies. It was eventually handed over to 2.Kompanie. This tank is also shown on page 22.

This Panther ausf A of 3.Kompanie, Panzer-Regiment 4 was abandoned near San Giovanni Incario after the fighting for Pontecorvo on 25 May 1944. The distinctive pattern of Zimmerit application is indicative of Panthers assembled by DEMAG. Note the stowage box on the rear hull, a common modification within this battalion. Another photograph of this tank is reproduced on page 54 and it is also shown on page 20 of the Camouflage & Markings section.

1 October 1944. US Army units attack Monte Battaglia, a part of the Gothic Line defences. The men of 44.Reichsgrenadier-Division Hoch und Deutschmeister manage to hold out for four days before retreating.

5 October 1944. Concerted assaults by American, British and Indian divisions force 10.Armee to withdraw toward Bologna.

20 October 1944. Monte Grande falls to the Americans and on the following day the British cross the Savio River.

23 October 1944. The British capture Monte Spaduro despite a dogged defence by men of Grenadier-Regiment 756 and Fallschirmjäger-Regiment 3.

5 November 1944. British troops capture Ravenna cutting the rail line to Bologna.

23 November 1944. Allied troops fight their way across the Cosina River but remain under constant artillery fire directed from the hills around Bologna.

25 November 1944. American and Brazilian troops attack Monte Belvedere and Monte Castello, south-west of Bologna, capturing both positions on the following day. But German counterattacks regain Monte Castello within hours and on 28 November the Brazilians are thrown off Monte Belvedere.

29 November 1944. A further attempt to take Monte Castello is repulsed. On the same day Allied troops take Faenza.

26 December 1944. After weeks of relative calm, the Axis units on the western sector of the Gothic Line launch a limited offensive between Massa and Lucca codenamed Wintergewitter, or Winter Storm. Two understrength Italian divisions with two battalions of Grenadier-Regiment 285 and two ad-hoc German battalions manage to penetrate the Allied lines and advance over 25 kilometres by the afternoon of the following day. They are eventually halted by fresh Indian units. Both sides take up defensive positions.

12 February 1945. The three remaining companies of Panzer-Regiment 4 are officially incorporated into Panzer-Regiment 26 as the regiment's first battalion.

20 February 1945. As the weather clears and the fighting resumes, American and Brazilian troops mount a full-scale offensive against German positions at Monte Castello and Monte Della Torraca which they had failed to secure in November.

8 March 1945. Unknown to either Hitler or OKW in Berlin, Generaloberst von Vietinghoff, by now the overall commander in Italy, and Obergruppenführer Karl Wolff secretly contact the Allies to discuss the possibility of surrender.

5 April 1945. British infantry units attack German positions near Lake Comacchio in preparation for a large-scale offensive.

6 April 1945. The Allies launch Operation Grapeshot, a major assault aimed at breaking into the Lombardy Plain and advancing to Bologna.

10 April 1945. A massive aerial bombardment of German positions along the Santerno River is conducted in preparation for a major assault towards Argenta. On the following day New Zealand and Polish troops cross the river.

12 April 1945. Indian troops cross the Santerno River as Panzergrenadier-Regiment 15 arrives to reinforce the German defenders.

14 April 1945. Panzergrenadier-Regiment 15 is able to hold up the British advance from the Santerno at Bastia and the Fossa Marina canal. On the same day elements of 29.Panzergrenadier-Division arrive as reinforcements. Hitler denies Vietinghoff's request to withdraw behind the Po River.

15 April 1945. US troops advance toward Bologna while the British launch an attack across the Fossa Marina canal.

17 April 1945. Brazilian troops capture the town of Montese. In two days of bitter fighting the British expand their bridgehead at the Fossa Marina canal by barely 900 metres.

18 April 1945. *The tanks of 29.Panzergrenadier-Division attack the British bridgehead north of the Fossa Marina canal but are beaten back.*

20 April 1945. *US Army units break through the German defensive lines and reach the Po River Valley north of Bologna which the Poles enter on the following day.*

23 April 1945. *Parts of 148.Infanterie-Division are sent towards Parma but find the city under the control of Italian partisans. Allied troops take Ferrara and Bondeno.*

24 April 1945. *British units attack across the Po River and advance to make contact with American troops. The last Panther tanks of I.Abteilung, Panzer-Regiment 26 are destroyed by their own crews.*

26 April 1945. *As units of the US Army capture Verona, uprisings begin in major Italian cities, notably Genoa and Milan.*

27 April 1945. *Fighting as infantry, the tank crews of Panzer-Regiment 26 defend a German field hospital at Crespano which is threatened by Italian partisans.*

28 April 1945. *Generaloberst von Vietinghoff dispatches a messenger from his headquarters at Bolzano toward the Allies lines seeking a ceasefire. On the same day the remnants of 148.Infanterie-Division are badly mauled by US armoured units at Fornovo di Taro, 10 kilometres south-east of Parma, and surrender en masse.*

29 April 1945. *British and American units link up near Padua, probably saving the German garrison which had been surrounded by Italian partisans.*

30 April 1945. *American units make contact with French forces near the Italo-French border. In Berlin, Hitler commits suicide.*

1 May 1945. *The German headquarters in Italy announces a cessation of hostilities and German troops begin surrendering. The last remnants of Panzer-Regiment 26 are interned near Brescia.*

Although technically beyond the remit of this book some mention should be made of the Pantherturm emplacements that were utilised in the fortifications which played such an important role in the German defence of the Italian peninsula. These installations were encountered as early as late 1943 in the fighting along the Hitler Line and by January 1945 a total of forty-eight turrets had been installed. The image above shows a rebuilt Panther ausf D turret mounted on an OT-Stahlunterstände near Rimini in September 1944. The OT-Stahlunterstände, which was basically a metal box, has been reinforced here with a concrete jacket. Below left is the final production version with its distinctive commander's hatch and 65mm thick roof. In addition, a number of tanks were simply buried up to the hull roof, allowing the driver's and radio operators hatches to be opened and closed. The photograph below right shows one such tank of 2.Kompanie, Panzer-regiment 4 which was disabled during the fighting for the Gothic Line. The deployment of the Pantherturm is explained further on pages 15 and 16.

The terrain of Italy and the length of the front, which was for the most part limited by the width of the peninsula, dictated the almost siege-like conditions of most operations. Large armoured engagements were rare and the campaign centred on a series of defensive lines. Nevertheless a number of Panzer and Panzergrenadier units were deployed to the Italian Front and some of the most successful fortifications were based on tank turrets. Set out below is a brief history of I.Abteilung, Panzer-Regiment 4, the only Panther-equipped unit to take part in the fighting, and an explanation of the Pantherturm bunkers which played an important role in the defensive battles. I have deliberately omitted any mention of SS-Panzer-Regiment 1, although that formation did spend time in northern Italy where it was re-equipped with Panther tanks, as it was not engaged in combat and had returned to the East by the end of 1943. Further details can be found in *Tank Craft 34: Panther Medium Tank German Army and Waffen SS Eastern Front, Summer, 1943.*

Notes

1. Each military district had a number of training and replacement units which served specific formations of the field army. This particular organisation was affiliated with Panzer-Regimenter 3, 4 and 33 and later schwere Panzer-Abteilung 507.

2. The German army's supply directorate.

Panzer-Regiment 4. One of the pre-war Panzer regiments, this unit was made up of two tank battalions and served in the Polish and French campaigns with 2.Panzer-Division.

As part of the reorganisation and expansion of the Panzer formations which took place in late 1940, the regiment was attached to the newly-formed 13.Panzer-Division and was engaged in the fighting on the Eastern Front from the first days of the German invasion in June 1941. In May 1942 a third battalion was created when III.Abteilung, Panzer-Regiment 29 was transferred to the division. But by February of 1943 it had been decided that the regiment would revert to the two battalion establishment and surplus personnel would be used to form a Panther abteilung for the division. It took some time to affect this change and it was not until 13 April 1943 that the tank crews, with Hauptmann Erich Schmidt in command, arrived at Mödling in Austria where they were attached to Panzer-Ersatz und Ausbildungs-Abteilung 4 (1).

On 5 May 1943 official tables of organisation were issued to the battalion, which was still referred to as III.Abteilung, but a shortage of personnel and an almost total lack of vehicles meant that these could not be implemented. In the following month Hauptmann Schmidt was notified that the battalion would be transferred to France to complete its training and by mid-September 1943, at almost full personnel strength but still without any tanks, the battalion was at Chateau Gonthier, south-west of Le Mans.

On 19 October 1943 the battalion was ordered to move to Truppenübungsplatz Mailly-le-Camp, the huge training centre east of Paris, where the crews were to receive their new tanks. At the same time the battalion was renamed I.Abteilung, Panzer-Regiment 4 and new tables of organisation were issued. This is explained in detail on page 62. At about the same time Hauptmann Schmidt left to take command of schwere Panzer-Abteilung 507 and was replaced by Major Förster.

On 13 December the first tanks were shipped by the Heereszeugamt (2) with thirty-eight vehicles dispatched before the end of the year. By the last week of January 1944 the battalion reported that a total of seventy-nine Panthers and two Bergepanther recovery tanks were on

Photographed in the streets of Rome in early February 1944, this Panther ausf A of I.Abteilung, Panzer-Regiment 4 is one of the five tanks allocated to the battalion's Auklärungs-Zug, identified by the number I14 just visible on the side of the turret. The presence of the pistol port on the turret side proves that this is not the tank with the same number shown in the photographs on page 13. Note the twin apertures for the TZF.12 sight on the gun mantlet and early-style aperture for the hull machine gun.

hand. Curiously, the 19 October order had stipulated that the battalion headquarters was to be organised *'ohne Aufklärungs-Zug'*, or without the usual reconnaissance platoon of five tanks, but the total number of Panthers received, and indeed photographic evidence, shows that they were on hand. Even so the figure of seventy-nine tanks was three more than the authorised allocation and it appears that the intention was to assign the surplus vehicles to the regimental headquarters when the battalion eventually returned to 13.Panzer-Division.

But within days I.Abteilung was ordered to the Italian Front and as it was accompanied by Stab, Panzer-Regiment 69, which was to act as the command and control staff for several armoured units that were to attack the Allied bridgehead at Anzio, that unit received the three extra tanks. In a report compiled in June 1944 the commander of I.Abteilung specifically mentions that these tanks were all command vehicles and it is generally assumed that they were the three tanks shipped on 24 January of the same year (see page 12).

The Panzerbefehlswagen command tanks of the battalion headquarters were based on the Panther ausf D and at least one had a very neatly applied coat of Zimmerit rendered with a texture made up of short horizontal strokes over which a grid has been worked. This pattern is most often associated with MAN-produced vehicles assembled in September and October 1943 (1). If this identification is correct this tank is either one of the very few Panther ausf D models to be coated with Zimmerit at the assembly plant or it was returned to the factory for conversion.

The majority of the Panther tanks that were with the battalion's four companies were Panther ausf A models but a number of Panther ausf D tanks were present. A photograph that can be dated to 2 March 1944, and was taken near Ponte Rotto on the Cisterna to Aprilia road, shows Panthers of 1.Kompanie and the cylindrical commander's cupola is clearly visible on one, although no other details are discernible. Photographs of other Panther ausf D tanks are shown on page 51.

In late April 1944 the personnel of Stab, Panzer-Regiment 69 returned to Germany and handed over their three Panzerbefehlswagen command tanks to I.Abteilung. This seems to have been the cause of a certain amount of reshuffling within the battalion and the command tanks may have been incorporated into the Aufklärungs-Zug while a number of that platoon's tanks were assigned to the companies. The photograph on page 13, taken in late May 1944 and showing a Panzerbefehlswagen numbered I14, would seem to support this (2).

The thirty-eight tanks shipped in May and June 1944 directly from Nachschub Italien (3) were most probably Panther ausf A models with some early production Panther ausf G versions. In a report dated 19 June 1944 the battalion commander states that of the seventy-six vehicles that left Germany in the previous January, plus the three Panzerbefehlswagen taken over from Stab, Panzer-Regiment 69, just two command tanks and thirteen gun tanks remained. Both command tanks and one Panther were with the battalion headquarters while the rest of the tanks were all assigned to 3.Kompanie. From the thirty-eight Panthers mentioned earlier, six tanks were appropriated by the headquarters of XIV.Panzerkorps before they reached the battalion and were used to cover the German withdrawal. Crewed by men from various units, three were lost to enemy fire and three were destroyed by their own crews for lack of spare parts. The remaining thirty-two tanks were shared between the battalion's 2.Kompanie and 4.Kompanie.

The replacement vehicles that were shipped to the battalion from Nachschub Südwest (4) in September and October 1944 were all Panther ausf G models. Photographs would suggest that a number of the September allocation were still coated in Zimmerit and all went to 1.Kompanie. The ten tanks in the October shipment, which did not arrive until the following month, were all later models without Zimmerit and some were almost certainly painted in one of the factory-applied camouflage schemes which were introduced from late August 1944. These ten vehicles were the last tanks the battalion received (5).

The battalion arrived in Italy on 30 January 1944 and as many of the country's railway bridges had been destroyed by Allied bombing, the tanks were forced to make the journey from Ficulle to the Anzio-Nettuno front on their own tracks. This resulted in numerous breakdowns and I.Abteilung probably fielded fewer than fifty Panthers when it was thrown into the attacks on the Allied bridgehead. The battalion remained in the area around Aprilia until March when the tanks were withdrawn to Cori, near Monte Cassino, and held as an operational reserve. During this time a number of tanks, possibly nine vehicles in total, which had been abandoned in the fighting around Aprilia were recovered. In May the battalion was back at the front but from this time rarely fought as a single unit with the four companies allocated individually to division and corps headquarters. The Panthers were able to take a heavy toll of Allied tanks but maintenance and recovery remained problematic. Towards the end of May, in the fighting between Ceprano and Roccasecca, on the Rome to

Notes

1. The photograph on page 3 depicts one of these command tanks while the profiles on pages 17 and 18 of the Camouflage & Markings section show two further examples.

2. Similarly, it is tempting to speculate that Panther 401, depicted on page 19 of the Camouflage & Markings section is the original I14.

3. Nachschub Italien was the supply chain directorate servicing units operating in the Mediterranean.

4. The renamed Nachschub Italien.

5. This does not include the two Bergepanther recovery vehicles that were shipped in November 1944 and a further two in February 1945.

Notes

1. This is Panther 401 shown on page 19.
2. One of these Panthers, numbered 401, is depicted on page 22 of the Camouflage & Markings section and shown in a photograph on page 5.

Naples highway, 4.Kompanie was able to destroy over thirty enemy tanks but lost more than half its strength including the company commander's tank (1).

By the end of the month the number of operational tanks had fallen to ten and the battalion commander reported that thirty vehicles had been destroyed by their own crews as they could not be recovered.

In June the remaining tanks were organised into three Kampfgruppen named for the company commanders. Five Panthers of 4.Kompanie, with a number of Tiger tanks and Ferdinand self-propelled guns, formed part of Gruppe Hinz and operated in the Montepulciano area along the Florence to Rome road. The tanks of Gruppe Reverchon, all from 2.Kompanie, conducted a rearguard action east of Lake Trasimene with the infantry units of 15.Panzergrenadier-Division and elements of 305.Infanterie-Division.

Gruppe Leichsenring, made up from the assets of 3.Kompanie, operated on the western edges of Lake Trasimene and in a single day, 28 June 1944, managed to destroy twelve enemy tanks. This feat was accomplished at a time when Oberleutnant Leichsenring's command did not include any operational vehicles. In mid-July, 3.Kompanie was able to take over a number of Pzkpfw IV tanks from the Panzer regiment of the Hermann Göring

division but these were in such poor condition that they were relinquished to II.Abteilung, Panzer-Regiment 26 by the end of the month. Gruppe Leichsenring and Gruppe Hinz were combined when the companies returned to the battalion.

By the beginning of August 1944, 1.Kompanie and 3.Kompanie were without tanks and the battalion could field just ten operational vehicles. But the remaining tanks were still capable of effective action and in a fierce firefight near Cerasa, about 20 kilometres south of Pesaro, which took place during the last week of August, the Panthers of 2.Kompanie were able to knock out twelve enemy tanks. Over the next few weeks the battalion was active in the Rimini area around Cattolica supporting the paratroopers of 1.Fallschirmjäger-Division and although twenty new tanks had arrived by 21 September 1944, these were all assigned to 1.Kompanie while the five surviving tanks of 4.Kompanie were all handed over to 2.Kompanie (2).

The crews of 3.Kompanie and 4.Kompanie, without tanks, were relocated to Arcigano, about 40 kilometres east of Verona, with the battalion's workshop while the battalion's 2.Kompanie supported 90.Panzergrenadier-Division in the Rimini area and 1.Kompanie was positioned near Santarcangelo di Romagna, 6 kilometres from the Adriatic coast. In early November

Photographed on the Via Apia, just outside the village of Tor Tre Ponti with the church of Santo Paolo Apostolo in the background, this Panther ausf A of 1.Kompanie, Panzer-Regiment 4 is often described as one of the tanks lost in the fighting of late May 1944. But it is more likely to be one of two Panthers disabled by mines and abandoned in the first week of March when the battalion was supporting an advance made by elements of the Hermann Göring division in this area. Note the short lengths of timber on the hull front. This tank is also shown in the Camouflage & Markings section on page 20.

Captured intact during the fighting on the Senger Line in May 1944, this Panzer ausf A of I.Abteilung, Panzer-Regiment 4 was assembeld before November 1943 and was probably one of the seventy-six original vehicles that the battalion took to Italy. Note the letterbox machine-gun aperture on the hull glacis and twin apertures for the TZF.12 gun sight on the main gun mantlet.

the tank crews of 3.Kompanie, which had been without tanks since the end of July, were sent to Mödling in Austria with orders to pick up new Panthers but no tanks were ever allocated. The men languished at Mödling until March 1945 when they were transferred to Fallinböstel in Germany to train on Panthers equipped with infrared night vision devices and never returned to the battalion. For the remainder of the year the battalion was held in reserve and operations across much of the front were halted due to the incessant rain which caused extensive flooding.

During the first week of January 1945 the tanks of 2.Kompanie were able to stop an Allied advance north of Alfonsine towards the Reno River and although the company was able to inflict heavy casualties on the enemy units it was badly battered and by 14 January was ordered to hand all its surviving tanks to 4.Kompanie. From the end of January until mid-April 1945 the entire 10.Armee front, from Bologna to the Adriactic coast, saw no major engagements and the battalion was withdrawn to Imola, just south of Bologna, and used the time to train the tank crews and repair its vehicles.

On 12 February 1945, I.Abteilung, Panzer-Regiment 4 was officially integrated into 26.Panzer-Division as the first battalion of Panzer-Regiment 26. At about this time the battalion could field one Panzerbefehlswagen command tank and one Panther with the headquarters while 1.Kompanie and 4.Kompanie had twelve tanks each. The tank crews of 2.Kompanie were acting as infantry and 3.Kompanie, it will be remembered, had been sent to Austria.

On 6 April 1945 an Allied offensive, codenamed Operation Grapeshot, was launched towards Bologna and the battalion was involved in heavy and costly rearguard actions between the Senio and Saterno rivers, south-west of Imola, under the command of I.Fallschirmkorps. By this time 2.Kompanie was fighting without tanks and the battalion could muster just twenty-two operational vehicles. The battalion managed to fall back to the Po River near Burana but found that there was no way to ferry the heavy tanks to the northern bank and during the early morning hours of Tuesday, 24 April 1945 the last Panthers were destroyed by their crews. Crossing the river with only a few wheeled vehicles the men gathered in Cenesalli and made their way, mostly on foot, to Vicenza, Arzignano and finally to Bassano di Grappa, on the Brenta River north of Padua, by the following Thursday. On 29 April 1945 all German units in Italy laid down their arms and the men of I.Abteilung, Panzer-Regiment 26, formerly Panzer-Regiment 4, passed into captivity.

I.ABTEILUNG, PANZER-REGIMENT 4. TANK STRENGTH AND ALLOCATIONS

Month	Allocations			Vehicle Status		
	Date Shipped	Quantity		Operational	In Repair	On Hand
		Panther	Bergepanther			
December 1943	13 December 1943	9				
	18 December 1943	16				
	19 December 1943	13				
	29 December 1943		2	38		38

The on hand and operational figures do not include the two Bergepanther recovery tanks. Most of the gun tanks were Panther ausf A with some Panther ausf D as explained in the main text.

January 1944	17 January 1943	8				
	18 January 1943	8				
	20 January 1943	16				
	23 January 1943	6				
	24 January 1943	3		50		79

The on hand and operational figures do not include the two Bergepanther recovery tanks. The three Panzerbefehlswagen (PzBefWg) command tanks with the battalion headquarters were all Panther ausf D models. Three further tanks, quite possibly the vehicles shipped on 24 January 1943, were assigned to Stab, Panzer-Regiment 69.

February 1944				30	37	67

In the attacks on the Anzio bridgehead a total of thirteen tanks either broke down or were disabled behind enemy lines or within range of enemy fire and could not be salvaged. At least four of these vehicles, possibly from 3.Kompanie and 1.Kompanie, were never recovered and were later photographed by the advancing Allies. The figure of thirty-seven tanks in repair includes seventeen vehicles in long-term repair, that is more than three weeks. A report compiled on 1 March 1944 stated that nine tanks had been completely written off since 31 January.

March 1944				55	12	67

The figure of twelve tanks in repair includes six vehicles in long-term repair. The status report for this month, compiled on 1 April 1944, makes no mention of the thirteen tanks stranded near or behind enemy lines and given the total loss of nine Panthers mentioned above, and the numbers presented in the returns for March, it would seem likely that four vehicles were recovered.

April 1944				64	6	70

During April, Stab, Panzer-Regiment 69 returned to Germany and the three tanks that were assigned to this unit in January or February were handed to the battalion.

May 1944	29 May 1944	8		6	18	24

On 23 May, two tanks of 1.Kompanie were lost and over the next few days five Panthers of 4.Kompanie were knocked out by enemy fire and another vehicles was later destroyed by its own crew. On 29 May the battalion reported that 'about' thirty Panthers had to be destroyed due to a lack of recovery equipment and spare parts. The eight tanks shipped on 29 May 1944 probably arrived on 4 June and were included in a report dated 14 June which gave seventeen tanks on hand with eleven of those being fully operational. The figure of eighteen tanks in repair is taken from the official report but is an estimate which of course effects the on hand number.

June 1944	3 June 1944	8				
	4 June 1944	10				
	5 June 1944	12		16	24	40

A report dated 19 June 1944 stated that of the three Panzerbefehlswagen (PzBefWg) and seventy-three gun tanks that were on hand in the previous February, plus the command tanks handed over by Stab, Panzer-Regiment 69, four of the PzBefWg had been lost while just thirteen tanks were still with the battalion. All of the latter were with 3.Kompanie. The report goes on to say that of the thirty-eight tanks shipped to the battalion, three were commandeered by XIV.Panzerkorps headquarters and never returned. Both Bergepanther recovery vehicles had been destroyed by their own crews.

July 1944				19	17	36

By the end of the month both 1.Kompanie and 3.Kompanie were without tanks. The battalion headquarters had two PzBefWg command vehicles and one Panther while 2.Kompanie and 4.Kompanie had sixteen and seventeen gun tanks respectively.

August 1944				10	20	30

1.Kompanie and 3.Kompanie were still without tanks. One of the PzBefWg command tanks was probably lost in this month. 2.Kompanie and 4.Kompanie had twelve and fifteen gun tanks respectively.

September 1944	13 September 1944	10				
	16 September 1944	10		17	15	32

The tanks allocated in this month arrived on 18 and 21 September and were all assigned to 1.Kompanie but it seems that one of these was lost before the end of the month. 2.Kompanie had ten tanks while 3.Kompanie was still without any tanks and 4.Kompanie was temporarily withdrawn from the front.

October 1944	31 October 1944	10		22	7	29

The tanks allocated in this month were the last replacements the battalion received. They probably arrived in the first week of November and were therefore not included in the strength report for October. The battalion spent most of October conducting a fighting withdrawal from Rimini to Cesena and the total on hand figure of twenty-nine strongly suggests that five tanks were lost during this time.

November 1944	18 November 1944		2	31	7	39

The tank crews of 3.Kompanie were sent to Mödling to pick up a number of new tanks but never returned to the battalion and were eventually transferred to Fallingböstel in Germany. Assuming that the October arrivals were included in this month's strength report it would seem that one tank was lost during November.

December 1944				20	12	32

THE PANTHER UNITS 13

Month	Allocations		Vehicle Status		
	Date Shipped	Quantity	Operational	In Repair	On Hand
January 1945			17	9	26

2.Kompanie handed all its remaining tanks to 4.Kompanie on 14 January. Note that the operational and on hand figures shown above were taken from a report dated 15 January 1945 and may not give a true picture of the battalion's strength at the end of the month.

February 1945	2 February 1945	2	21	5	26

The battalion was permanently attached to 26.Panzer-Division and renamed I.Abteilung, Panzer-Regiment 26. The headquarters had one PzBefWg and one Panther while 1.Kompanie and 4.Kompanie were each equipped with twelve tanks.

March 1945			22	3	25

The headquarters had one PzBefWg and one Panther while 1.Kompanie and 4.Kompanie had thirteen and ten tanks respectively.

April 1945					

Accurate figures for April are not available but the majority of the battalion's tanks were probably lost before the last surviving Panthers were destroyed by their own crews during the early morning hours of 24 April near Burana, north-west of Ferrara, at the Po River crossing.

The official caption of this US Army Signal Corps photograph states that this Panzerbefehlswagen V ausf A was found abandoned outside San Giovanni Incario on 26 May 1944. The image was passed by the censor for publication on 29 June 1944 meaning that it could not have been taken after that date and that the caption is probably correct. This tank was also filmed by the British and in that film, and the smaller photgraph inset here, the tank's number can be seen to be I14. This is, however, not the vehicle shown driving through Rome on page 8 and the tank shown here may have been one of the Panzerbefehlswagen handed over by Stab, Panzer-Regiment 69 when that unit returned to Germany. The stencilled notations on the gun cleaning rod tube are explained in detail on page 23.

Said to have been photographed during the late summer of 1944, this Panzerbefehlswagen V ausf A was assembled before November 1943 when the Kugelblende machine-gun mount was introduced into production. Note also the pistol port on the turret side which was deleted in the following month. Presumably this tank replaced the vehicle shown on page 17 which has the same turret number and this command tank may be another of the vehicles handed over from Stab, Panzer-Regiment 69. The pattern created by the texture worked into the Zimmerit has often been interpreted as that employed by DEMAG but it is in fact a method used for a short period in September and October 1943 by MAN and was similar to that seen on Tiger I tanks. The Panther ausf A in the background is the tank shown in the photograph on page 53.

Manufactured by Daimler-Benz, probably in January 1944, this Panther ausf A is one of a number of tanks that were buried in this manner as part of the Gothic Line defences. It is likely that 10.Armee headquarters gave permission for four tanks of I.Abteilung, Panzer-Regiment 4 to be used in this manner and it is known that eight prospective sites were inspected but I have been unable to determine the exact number involved. This tank, formerly of the battalion's 2.Kompanie, was emplaced near Pesaro above the Foglia River valley. Note that the Zimmerit has been applied to the commander's cuopla.

Designed initially for use on the Eastern Front, bunkers fitted with a Panther turret were employed extensively in Italy. A prefabricated steel box, referred to as an OT-Stahlunterstand, served as a crew compartment and this was buried in a suitable position and surrounded by concrete reinforcing. In an effort to deliver a number of bunkers to Italy as quickly as possible new Panther ausf A turrets, minus the hydraulic traverse, were fitted to the first versions. Later, the turrets of rebuilt Panther ausf D models were used and a modified version with 65mm thick roof armour, new commander's hatch and Nahverteidigungswaffe close-defence weapon was produced. These versions were referred to as Pantherturm I. A model designed to be mounted on a concrete bunker, the Pantherturm II (Betonsockel), was develpoed in late 1944 using turrets that were surplus to the Stahlbunker programme (1).

On 29 April 1944 the headquarters of 10.Armee was authorised to form a Festungs-Kompanie to defend the Senger-Riegel, or Senger Line, defences which was a branch of the Gustav Line running from Monte Cairo, just behind Monte Cassino, through the Liri Valley to Terracina on the coast (2). The company was to control twelve Pantherturm and each turret was manned by a commander, gunner and loader. The officers were appointed by the Personal-Amt of OKH while the NCOs and other ranks were supposed to be seconded from the Panzer-Ersatz-Kompanie of 15.Panzergrenadier-Division but in reality the men came from artillery, infantry and even Fallschirmjäger units. Regardless of

their origin they remained under the auspices of the Generalinspekteur der Panzertruppen. Official establishments were issued by the Organisations-Abteilung of OKH and these were almost certainly KstN Festungs-Kompanie (12 Panthertürme) von 8 May 1944, although the first time this document is mentioned specifically is in the following November.

By 11 May 1944 the men of Festungs-Pantherturm-Kompanie were in position and subordinated to the command of LI.Gebirgskorps. A report of 19 May 1944 states that each turret was furnished with 200 rounds of ammunition and a further 1,000 rounds were held in reserve. On the same day the Allies began their first attacks on the Senger Line. In combat these Panther turrets proved devastating and a single emplacement located near Piedmonte San Germano and commanded by Gefreiter Herbert Fries, formerly of Fallschirm-Panzeräger-Abteilung 1, was credited with the destruction of twenty enemy tanks in just three days of fighting (3).

By late May the Senger Line had been completely overrun and the Germans withdrew to the Caesar C Line which was largely incomplete and then to the Trasimine Line which they abandoned by the end of June 1944. Despite Hitler's insistence that no ground be lost, these positions were merely intended to slow the Allies while the defences of the Gothic Line could be reinforced. The latter was originally to contain twelve Panther turret installations but in in July 1944 the headquarters of XIV.Panzerkorps was granted permission to form a second

Notes

1. The description of this equipment offered here is, of necessity, extremely basic and a more detailed examination of the technical aspects of these bunkers may be included in a future title.
2. The Senger Line of fortified positions is probably better known as the Hitler Line and is shown as such on our map on page 2. The name was changed by the Führer's express order, probably to avoid any adverse propaganda should the defences not be held.
3. The number of tanks destroyed varies in some accounts but the figure of twenty given here is taken from the recommendation for Gefreiter Fries' Ritterkreuz.

This Pantherturm I is based on a new Panther ausf A turret and is typical of the emplacements encountered on the Hitler Line in mid-1944. Note the twin apertures for the TZF.12 gun sight and cast commander's cupola.

Said to have been photographed near Senigallia, south-east of Rimini, in June 1944 this Pantherturm I was part of the Gothic Line defences. Note the commander's hatch with single swivelling periscope identifying the final production version of the turret.

Notes

1. There is some confusion over the number of tanks taken from Panzer-Regiment 4. The Kriegstagbuch of Festungs-Pionier Stab 16 mentions that in a meeting held on 22 July 1944 Oberstleutnant Pflum, the Panzerabwehr-Offizier of 10.Armee, had inspected prospective sites for eight stationary Panthers and five Panther turrets. Pflum also stated that two immobile Panthers were at that time in Cesena, north-west of Rimini.

2. By January 1945 this total had been increased to thirty-seven.

company and this was referred to as Festungs (Panther-Kompanie) 2 while the original unit was renamed Festungs (Panther-Kompanie) 1. In addition, on 19 July, 10.Armee headquarters ordered that unrepairable Panthers from I.Abteilung, Panzer-Regiment 4 be installed as static defences on the Gothic Line (1).

This was the last major line of defence before the Alps and was intended to be made up of two bands of strong fortifications, Green I and Green II, but large stretches of the German front line were still under preparation when the fighting commenced. As late as 28 August 1944, three days after the first Allied attacks began along the Metauro River, headquarters of 10.Armee reported that just four Panther turret positions for Festungs (Panther-Kompanie) 1 had been completed while eighteen were under construction and a further seven were planned. Festungs (Panther-Kompanie) 2 was tasked with holding the passes at the western end of the Green Line and may have been able to employ as many as seven turrets in the battle but the exact number is unclear. The immobile tanks of Panzer-Regiment 4 were in the eastern section of the German defences near Pesaro on the Adriatic coast.

By 22 September 1944 Festungs (Panther-Kompanie) 1 had been withdrawn from the front line to prepare for Operation Herbstnebel, the planned retreat to the Alpine foothills and the Blue Line. Also known as the Voralpenstellung, the Blue Line was the last German defensive line in

Italy. Running from the Adriatic coast near the mouth of the Tagliamento River, the line was anchored on Belluno and from there ran in an arc south to Asiago, about 30 kilometres north of Vicenza, then to the northern edge of Lake Garda before curving towards the north and the Stelvio Pass on the Swiss border. Its main purpose was to protect the Ljubljana Gap beyond which lay Austria and Czechoslovakia.

On 19 November 1944 a total of twelve new companies were formed and numbered in the 1200 series. Festungs (Pantherturm) Kompanien 1209 and 1210 were allocated to Oberbefhlshaber (OB) Südwest, the overall commander in Italy. An OKW memo dated 26 November ordered that a total of thirty Panther turrets were to be sent to OB Südwest by mid-December (2) and companies were to be ready for deployment by the last day of December 1944.

The first deliveries of nineteen turrets were caught in air raids at Wörgel in northern Austria and although the damage was relatively light an attempt to recover them could not be made before early April 1945. Some supplies did get through including four Pantherturm II turrets intended for Ospedaletto, north of Udine, and seven for Asiago. On 9 April 1945 Festungs (Panther-Kompanie) 1 and Festungs (Panther-Kompanie) 2 were located at Vittorio Veneto, south of Belluno, while Festungs (Pantherturm) Kompanie 1209 was at Gorizia, on the present-day Slovenian border, and Festungs (Pantherturm) Kompanie 1210 was nearby.

1. Pzkpfw V ausf A. 2.Kompanie, Panzer-Regiment 5. Rome, February 1944. This tank was assembled at some time between September 1943, when Zimmerit was introduced, and December of the same year when the pistol port on the turret side was dropped from production. Not visible here are the twin apertures for the TZF.12 sight at the front of the gun manlet. Note that the tube for the gun cleaning rods is held in place by the very first pattern brackets. The coating of Zimmerit has been applied in the pattern indicative of tanks produced by Daimler-Benz.

2. Panzerbefehlswagen V ausf D. Stab, I.Abteilung, Panzer-Regiment 4. Anzio-Nettuno Front, early spring 1944. The battalion headquarters had three of these early production models on hand and all were probably marked like this. Our photographs (3 and 4) show that the large numbers were carried on both the turret rear and sides. Note the large armoured cap (5) that protected the submersible equipment. These were fitted to very few tanks. Note that traces of Zimmerit are just visible on the right side stowage bin.

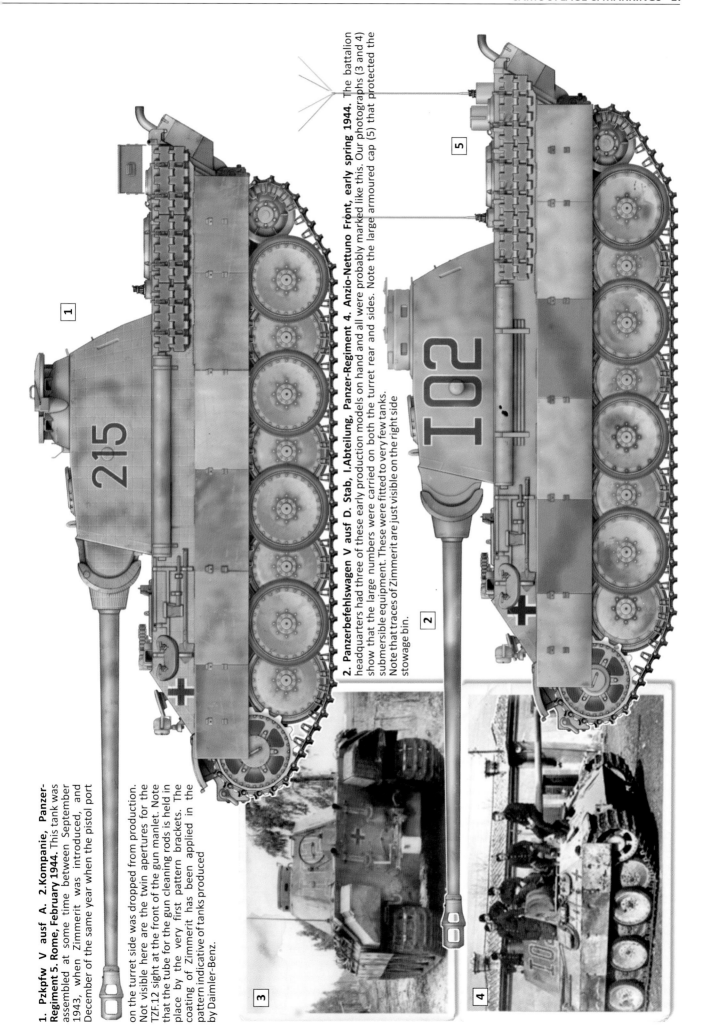

1. Panzerbefehlswagen V ausf D. Stab, I.Abteilung, Panzer-Regiment 4. Anzio-Nettuno Front, spring 1944. It is generally assumed that the three command tanks of the battalion headquarters lacked Zimmerit but the series of photographs on which this illustration is based clearly show

a comprehensive coating of the anti-magnetic mine paste applied in the first pattern employed by MAN, made up of short vertical strokes over which a grid was worked into the paste. Note the very early pattern wide fender which has been painted white (2). The plug welded over the aperture for the coaxial machine gun is clearly visible in the photograph used to create this illustration as is the pattern of Zimmerit shown here (3).

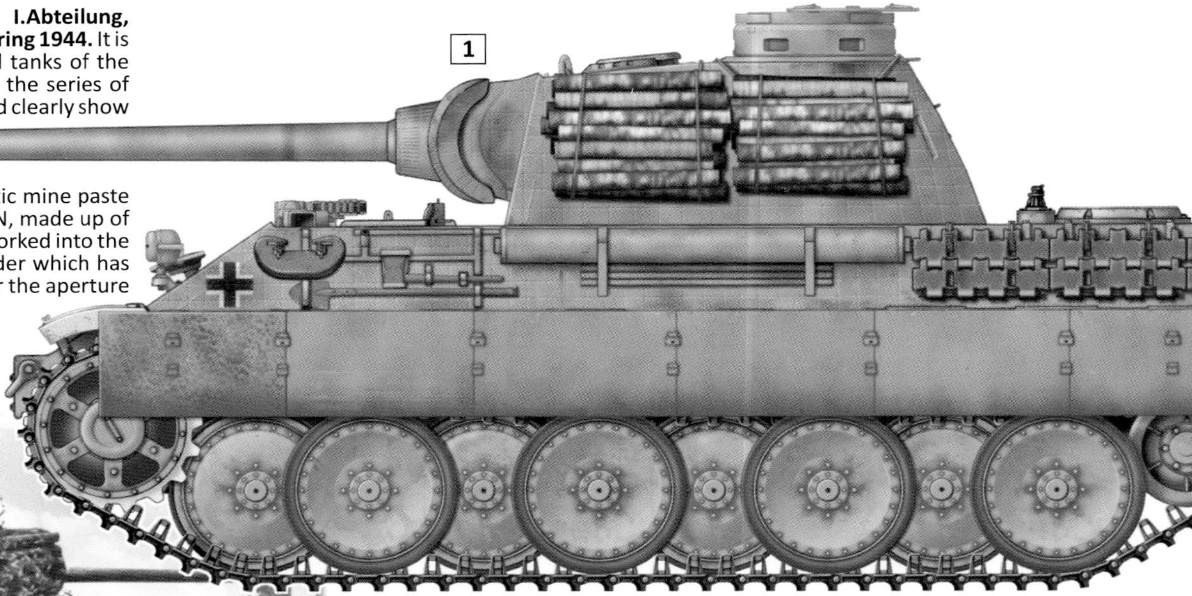

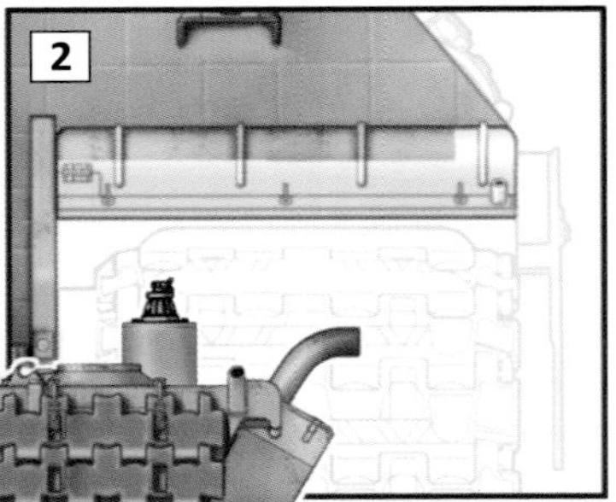

4. Pzkpfw V ausf A. 1.Kompanie, Panzer-Regiment 4. Anzio-Nettuno Front, spring 1944. This tank was photographed from several angles, possibly just before the battalion went into action for the first time, which has allowed us to create an accurate representation of its appearance. The company number is very neatly rendered, which was not always the case, to the rear and both sides of the turret. The numbers

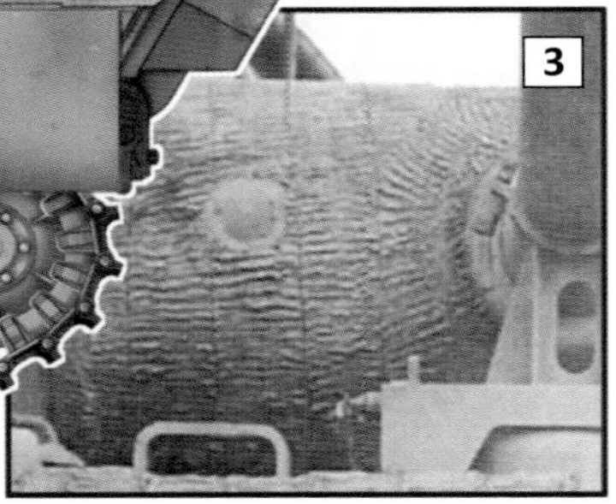

were red with a thin white outline as confirmed by surviving colour images. Note that the application of camouflage seems to have been limited to the hull Schürzen and gun barrel and this may have been a common feature of the battalion's Panthers. Note also the 15-ton jack (5) in its horizontal bracket on the hull rear plate below the exhaust manifolds. Another photograph of this tank is reproduced on the inside front cover.

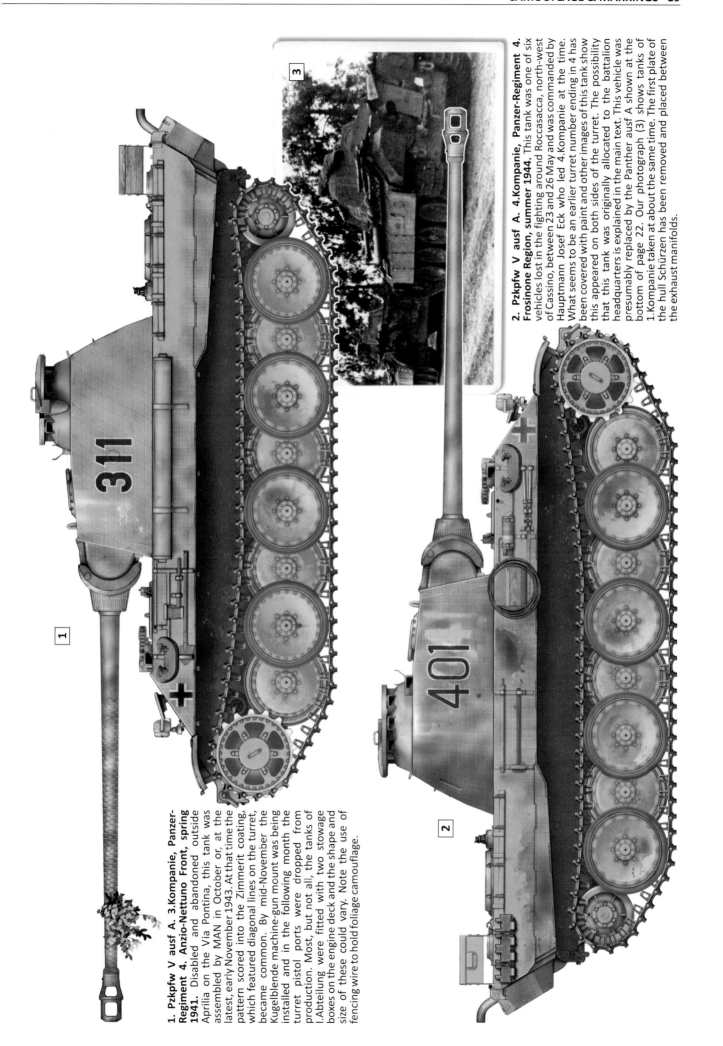

1. Pzkpfw V ausf A. 3.Kompanie, Panzer-Regiment 4. Anzio-Nettuno Front, spring 1941. Disabled and abandoned outside Aprilia on the Via Pontina, this tank was assembled by MAN in October or, at the latest, early November 1943. At that time the pattern scored into the Zimmerit coating, which featured diagonal lines on the turret, became common. By mid-November the Kugelblende machine-gun mount was being installed and in the following month the turret pistol ports were dropped from production. Most, but not all, the tanks of I.Abteilung were fitted with two stowage boxes on the engine deck and the shape and size of these could vary. Note the use of fencing wire to hold foliage camouflage.

2. Pzkpfw V ausf A. 4.Kompanie, Panzer-Regiment 4. Frosinone Region, summer 1944. This tank was one of six vehicles lost in the fighting around Roccasacca, north-west of Cassino, between 23 and 26 May and was commanded by Hauptmann Josef Eck who led 4.Kompanie at the time. What seems to be an earlier turret number ending in 4 has been covered with paint and other images of this tank show this appeared on both sides of the turret. The possibility that this tank was originally allocated to the battalion headquarters is explained in the main text. This vehicle was presumably replaced by the Panther ausf A shown at the bottom of page 22. Our photograph (3) shows tanks of 1.Kompanie taken at about the same time. The first plate of the hull Schürzen has been removed and placed between the exhaust manifolds.

1. Pzkpfw V ausf A. 1.Kompanie, Panzer-Regiment 4. Anzio-Nettuno Front, spring 1944. At this time the Panther tanks of the battalion carried bundles of small logs on the turret sides and at least this tank had similar pieces fixed to the hull glacis (2). They would have afforded no protection from anti-tank rounds and were almost certainly carried to help extricate the vehicle if it became bogged down. Note the early pattern brackets holding the tube for the gun cleaning rods. This version was gradually phased out of production from August 1943. This Panther is also shown and discussed on page 14.

3. Pzkpfw V ausf A. 3.Kompanie, Panzer-Regiment 4. Cassino Front, spring 1944. Photographed near the town of San Giovanni Incarico, this tank's coat of Zimmerit is textured in the pattern of short vertical ridges (4) that was indicative of DEMAG-produced vehicles. The construction of the wooden stowage boxes, and the brackets that held them in place, are visible in our photograph (5). Gun barrels were coated in a very dark heat-resistant laquer and often left unpainted. Photographs of this tank are reproduced on pages 6 and 54.

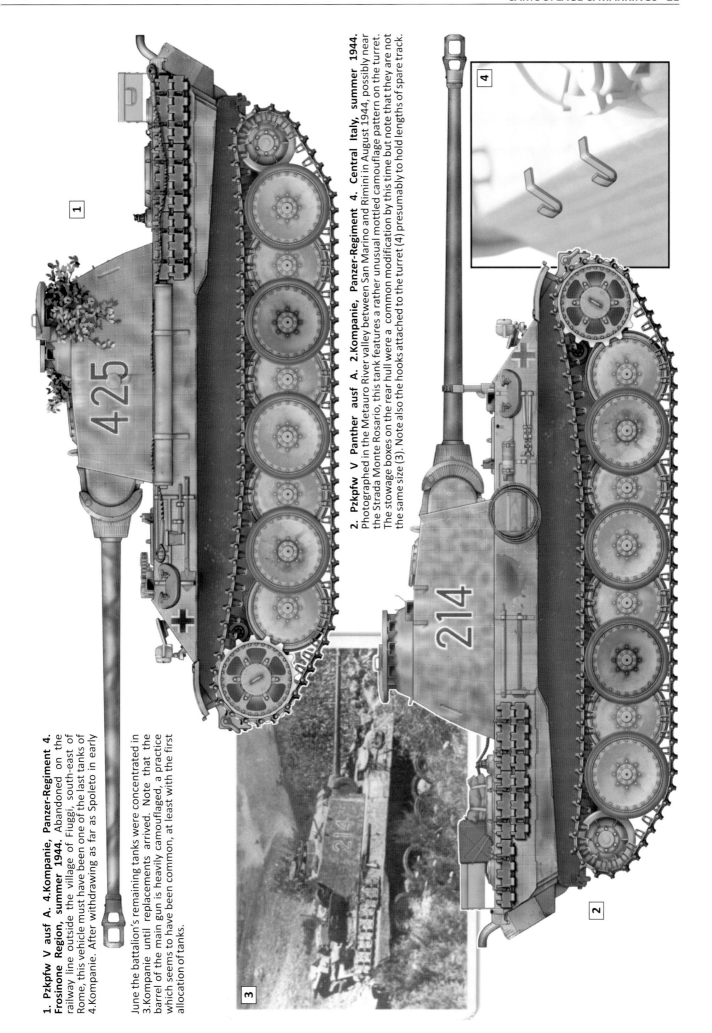

1. Pzkpfw V ausf A. 4.Kompanie, Panzer-Regiment 4. Frosinone Region, summer 1944. Abandoned on the railway line outside the village of Fiuggi, south-east of Rome, this vehicle must have been one of the last tanks of 4.Kompanie. After withdrawing as far as Spoleto in early

June the battalion's remaining tanks were concentrated in 3.Kompanie until replacements arrived. Note that the barrel of the main gun is heavily camouflaged, a practice which seems to have been common, at least with the first allocation of tanks.

2. Pzkpfw V Panther ausf A. 2.Kompanie, Panzer-Regiment 4. Central Italy, summer 1944. Photographed in the Metauro River valley between San Marino and Rimini in August 1944, possibly near the Strada Monte Rosario, this tank features a rather unusual mottled camouflage pattern on the turret. The stowage boxes on the rear hull were a common modification by this time but note that they are not the same size (3). Note also the hooks attached to the turret (4) presumably to hold lengths of spare track.

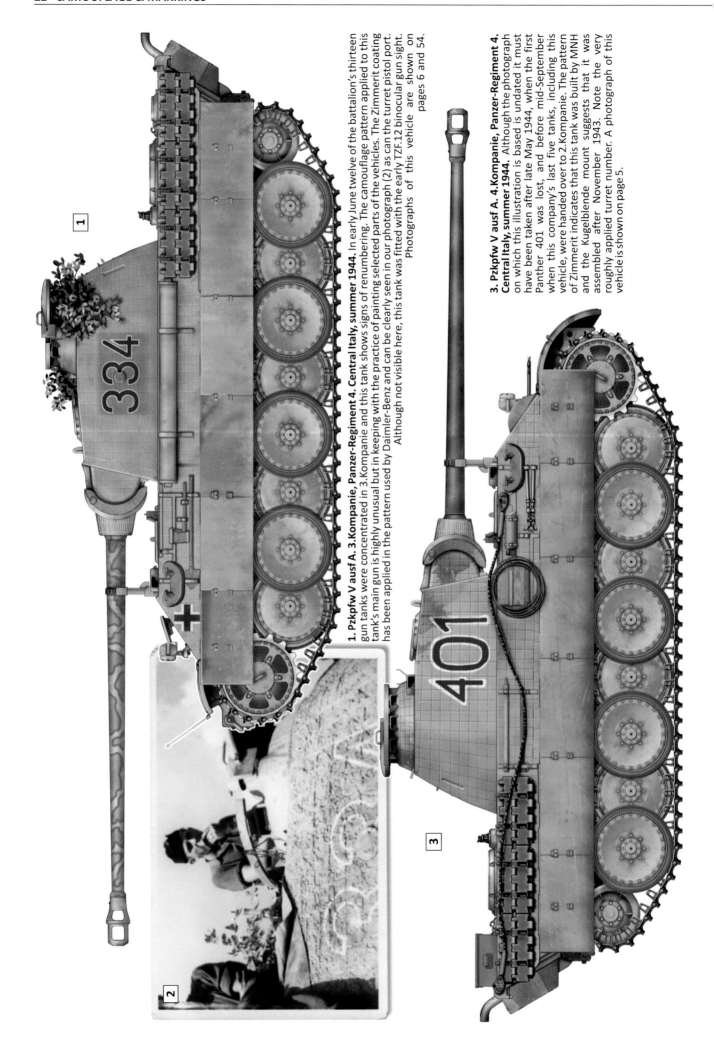

1. Pzkpfw V ausf A. 3.Kompanie, Panzer-Regiment 4. Central Italy, summer 1944. In early June twelve of the battalion's thirteen gun tanks were concentrated in 3.Kompanie and this tank shows signs of renumbering. The camouflage pattern applied to this tank's main gun is highly unusual but in keeping with the practice of painting selected parts of the vehicles. The Zimmerit coating has been applied in the pattern used by Daimler-Benz and can be clearly seen in our photograph (2) as can the turret pistol port. Although not visible here, this tank was fitted with the early TZF.12 binocular gun sight. Photographs of this vehicle are shown on pages 6 and 54.

3. Pzkpfw V ausf A. 4.Kompanie, Panzer-Regiment 4. Central Italy, summer 1944. Although the photograph on which this illustration is based is undated, it must have been taken after late May 1944, when the first Panther 401 was lost, and before mid-September when this company's last five tanks, including this vehicle, were handed over to 2.Kompanie. The pattern of Zimmerit indicates that this tank was built by MNH and the Kugelblende mount suggests that it was assembled after November 1943. Note the very roughly applied turret number. A photograph of this vehicle is shown on page 5.

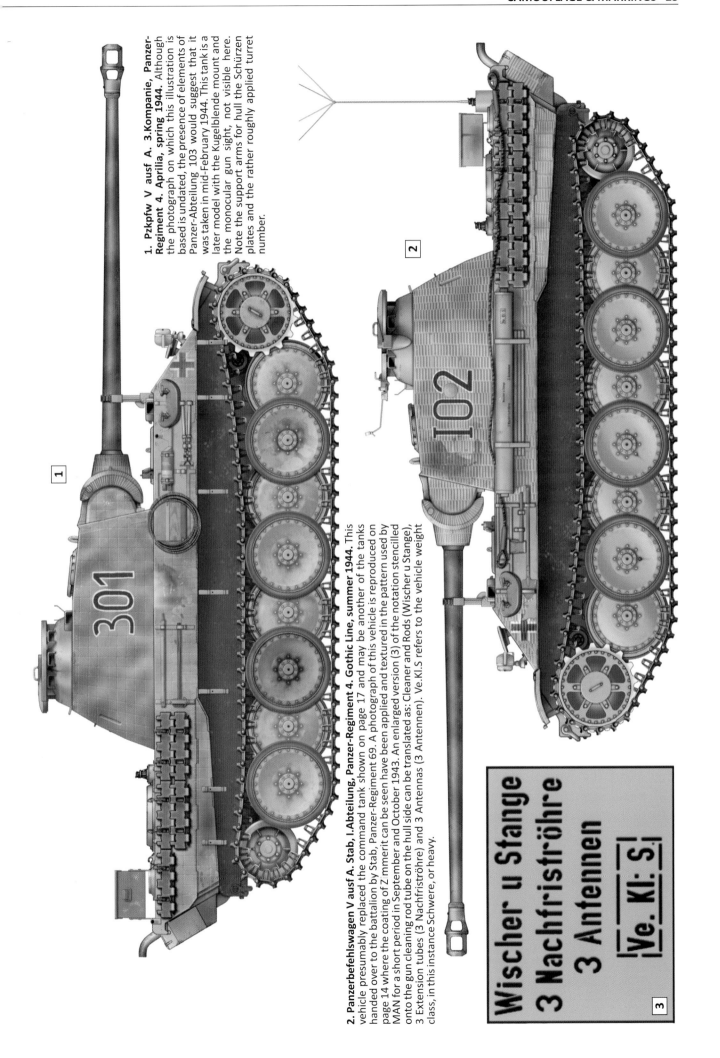

1. Pzkpfw V ausf A. 3.Kompanie, Panzer-Regiment 4. Aprilia, spring 1944. Although the photograph on which this illustration is based is undated, the presence of elements of Panzer-Abteilung 103 would suggest that it was taken in mid-February 1944. This tank is a later model with the Kugelblende mount and the monocular gun sight, not visible here. Note the support arms for hull the Schürzen plates and the rather roughly applied turret number.

2. Panzerbefehlswagen V ausf A. Stab, I.Abteilung, Panzer-Regiment 4. Gothic Line, summer 1944. This vehicle presumably replaced the command tank shown on page 17 and may be another of the tanks handed over to the battalion by Stab, Panzer-Regiment 69. A photograph of this vehicle is reproduced on page 14 where the coating of Zimmerit can be seen have been applied and textured in the pattern used by MAN for a short period in September and October 1943. An enlarged version (3) of the notation stencilled onto the gun cleaning rod tube on the hull side can be translated as: Cleaner and Rods (Wischer u Stange), 3 Extension tubes (3 Nachfriströhre) and 3 Antennas (3 Antennen). Ve.Kl.S refers to the vehicle weight class, in this instance Schwere, or heavy.

Wischer u Stange
3 Nachfriströhre
3 Antennen
Ve. Kl. S

1. Pzkpfw V ausf A. Stab, 4.Kompanie, Panzer-Regiment 4. Central Italy, summer 1944. Assembled by MAN, this tank is coated in Zimmerit that has been applied with the texture commonly seen on that manufacturer's vehicles including the diagonal lines on the turret side. Clearly visible in our photograph (2) are the vertically positioned 20-ton jack and the towing coupling welded to the engine access hatch. These features identify this vehicle as one of the May or June 1944 replacements and from this I have assumed the Kugelblende mount.

3. Pzkpfw V ausf A. 4.Kompanie, Panzer-Regiment 4. Central Italy, early autumn 1944. Abandoned near Montescudo-Monte Colombo, a collection of villages near San Marino, this tank is one of the original Panthers that arrived in Italy in February 1944. After supporting the grenadiers of 198.Infanterie-Division in this area, the company handed its remaining tanks to 2.Kompanie and was without vehicles for some time. The pattern of Zimmerit is quite clear in the photograph used to create this illustration and identifies this as an MHN-produced vehicle. From about this time the stowage boxes on the engine deck are seen less frequently and were probably not fitted to replacements. The practice of not repainting the barrel of the main gun was almost universal within this battalion.

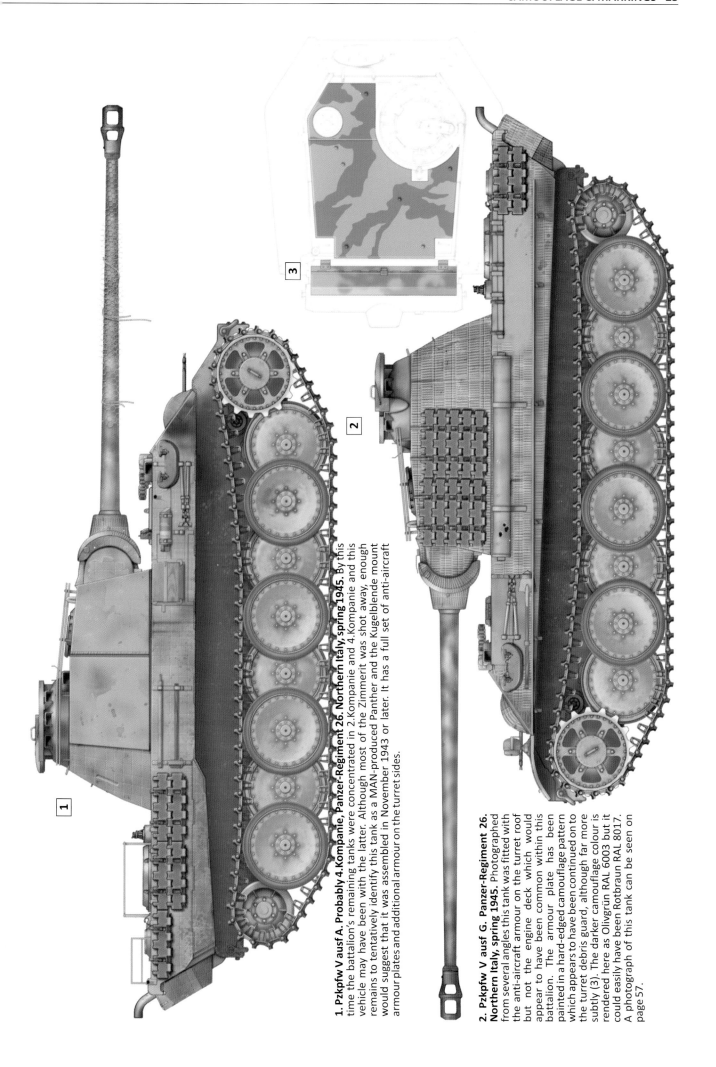

1 **2** **3**

1. Pzkpfw V ausf A. Probably 4.Kompanie, Panzer-Regiment 26. Northern Italy, spring 1945. By this time the battalion's remaining tanks were concentrated in 2.Kompanie and 4.Kompanie and this vehicle may have been with the latter. Although most of the Zimmerit was shot away, enough remains to tentatively identify this tank as a MAN-produced Panther and the Kugelblende mount would suggest that it was assembled in November 1943 or later. It has a full set of anti-aircraft armour plates and additional armour on the turret sides.

2. Pzkpfw V ausf G. Panzer-Regiment 26. Northern Italy, spring 1945. Photographed from several angles this tank was fitted with the anti-aircraft armour on the turret roof but not the engine deck which would appear to have been common within this battalion. The armour plate has been painted in a hard-edged camouflage pattern which appears to have been continued on to the turret debris guard, although far more subtly (3). The darker camouflage colour is rendered here as Olivgrün RAL 6003 but it could easily have been Rotbraun RAL 8017. A photograph of this tank can be seen on page 57.

1. Pzkpfw V ausf G. 4.Kompanie, Panzer-Regiment 26. Northern Italy, spring 1945. Photographed in the village of Sesto Imolese, almost exactly half way between Bologna and Ravenna, this tank was assembled in October 1944 when the Kampfraumheizung, or crew compartment heater, was introduced into production and was almost certainly one of ten replacement vehicles the battalion received in the same month.

Above: This tank and Panther 434 (2), with which it was photographed, were part of the 31 October 1944 consignment of ten replacement vehicles. From late August tanks were painted in a more or less standardised camouflage scheme before leaving the factories and what may be traces of what is referred to today as the Ambush Scheme, characterised by small dots of contrasting colour, are faintly visible in our photographs (3 and 4). This camouflage pattern is indicative of tanks assembled by Daimler-Benz and was very short lived, being discontinued in late September 1944. This tank has the additional armour plates on the turret roof and engine deck but the cover for the Kampfraumheizung appears to also have metal sides. The crew compartment heater of tank 434 had no cover at all.

5. Pzkpfw V ausf A. 4.Kompanie, Panzer-Regiment 26. Northern Italy, summer 1945. This vehicle was probably photographed after the end of the war but may be one of the thirty-eight replacements the battalion received in May and June 1944 before the application Zimmerit was discontinued. Note the Kugelblende machine-gun mount indicating that this tank was assembled after November 1943. In common with most of the battalion's Panthers at this time it has the spaced armour plates fitted to the turret roof and I have assumed the armour on the engine deck although it is not visible in the photograph on which this illustration is based.

PANTHER
AUSF G
1/72 SCALE
STEVE SHRIMPTON

Steve's model represents one of the earlier production Panther ausf G tanks assembled before mid-September 1944 when the application of Zimmerit was discontinued. Examples of this version were probably included in the May and June 1944 shipments to I.Abteilung, Panzer-Regiment 4, as this formation was known before February 1945 when it was incorporated into Panzer-Regiment 26. It is based on the Dragon Models' 1/72 scale kit, shown at left, and finished with photo-etched detail sets from Voyager Model.

Once the model was completely assembled it was first coated in grey primer and then Humbrol 103 Cream which, after extensive weathering, gave the appearance of Dunkelgelb.

The fully built replica ready for painting. Details are a mix of kit parts, photo-etched pieces and scratch-built sections.

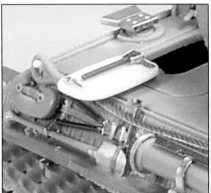

At right: Another view of the fully assembled model. Above, from left to right: The scratch-built jack block and resin fire extinguisher, the open driver's hatch and the commander's cupola with photo-etched parts.

The completed model after weathering with crew figures in place. Note the large bolts holding the turret armour in place, the hole for the Nahverteidigungswaffe close defence weapon and small cut away section in front of the cupola for the vane sight. Small details, such as the tools, were painted with a fine brush and Steve made the foliage camouflage from scrap.

A rear view of Steve's completed model. The arrangement of the additional turret armour is shown to good effect here. Note the 20-ton jack in its vertical bracket and the sheet metal covers for the exhaust pipes.

PANTHER
AUSF G
1/35 SCALE

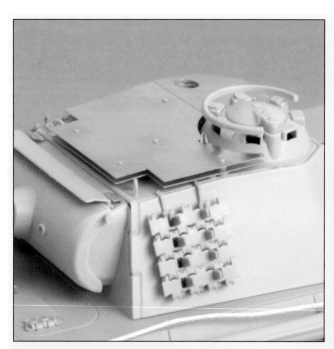 

James' model is based on the Italeri 1/35 scale kit which comes with photo-etched parts to build the anti-aircraft armour, shown above, that was fitted to the tanks of I.Abteilung, Panzer-Regiment 26 during the winter of 1944-1945. The Italeri offering is based on the suspension and lower hull of the company's 1993 Panther ausf A model with new parts added in 2012 to build a Panther ausf G. James found the detail, from the poorly rendered wheel bolts and tracks to the indistinct moulding of the pioneer tools, was mediocre at best but decided to build the kit using the parts provided. In his own words: 'There is a certain allure in trying to build and improve upon old kits and giving them a respectable paint job despite their quirks'.

Once built, the model was finished in Tamiya Acrylics XF-88 Dark Yellow, XF-89 Dark Green, and XF-90 Red Brown. These later model tanks, shipped to the battalion in October 1944, were almost certainly painted in one of the factory-applied camouflage schemes, as James has replicated here, and the possible patterns are discussed further in the Camouflage & Markings section of this book.

Below: The anti-aircraft armour plates, as supplied with the kit, fitted to the engine deck and turret roof. The lengths of spare track carried on the turret sides was also a common modification made to the tanks of this battalion.

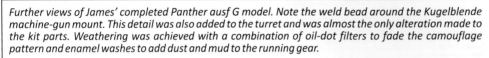

Further views of James' completed Panther ausf G model. Note the weld bead around the Kugelblende machine-gun mount. This detail was also added to the turret and was almost the only alteration made to the kit parts. Weathering was achieved with a combination of oil-dot filters to fade the camouflage pattern and enamel washes to add dust and mud to the running gear.

PANTHER
AUSF D
1/35 SCALE
BRETT GREEN

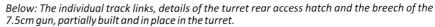

Brett Green will be familiar to many readers as the editor of Model Military International Magazine and the man behind Missing Lynx, a website dedicated to armour modelling. Brett is also an accomplished modeller and has based this project on Tamyia's Panther ausf D kit, first released in 2015. The Tamiya track upgrade set, the metal barrel of the main gun and the photo-etched parts depicting the engine grilles shown on the following pages are all available separately. The command antenna set, which includes a jig to help recreate the 'star' section, is from Tasca.

Below: The individual track links, details of the turret rear access hatch and the breech of the 7.5cm gun, partially built and in place in the turret.

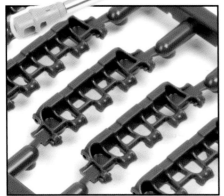

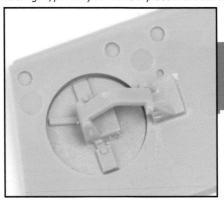

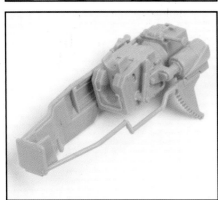

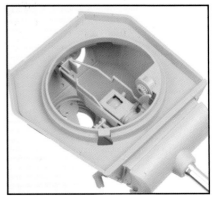

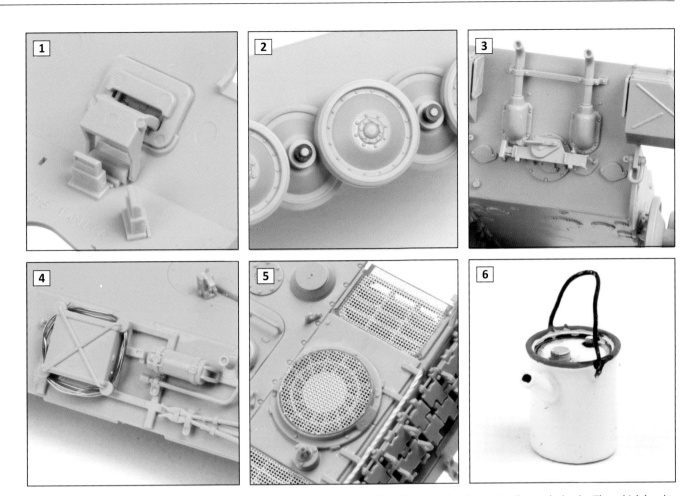

Above: 1. The hull interior showing the driver's visor and periscope. 2. The road wheels. The vehicle's axles are separate parts, each keyed with a large locating hole and a raised peg. This enables the builder to pose the tank on uneven ground by snipping off the pegs and repositioning the axles. 3. The exhausts and vertically-positioned jack. 4. The wooden jack block with the first pattern bracket. 5. The photo-etched covers for the engine deck louvres and intakes. 6. The ubiquitous container that will eventually hang from the jack.

At right: A trial assembly of the model. Brett removed the wheels and tracks as a single piece and replaced them once the hull and turret was painted.

Below: The set of waterslide transfers depicting Panther tanks of I.Abteilung, Panzer-Regiment 4 from Echelon Fine Decals

Above: After the camouflage colours were applied, the model received two airbrushed coats of Future Floor Polish. This served the dual purpose of delivering a glossy surface for the markings, and sealing the model prior to weathering.

At left: The hull and turret were painted with the running gear removed. Determining the camouflage from available photographs was difficult and in the end Brett opted for a heavily thinned dark green over a Dunkelgelb base with traces of red brown along the length of the side skirts. For the primary coat Brett mixed roughly equal quantities of Tamiya XF-59 Desert yellow, XF-60 Dark Yellow and XF-2 Flat White and then added more white for a paler coating on the horizontal surfaces and the top of the vehicle sides.

Below: The painted crew figures in place. These are included with the kit.

The fully assembled and painted model. The transfers were flattened with Solvaset and as the big red and white characters had to fit over several raised and recessed surface features, as well as overlapping a couple of hatches and pistol ports, Brett cut them and repainted the missing areas with a fine brush. The model was treated with a coat of MIG Productions Brown Filter, followed by a substantial wash using Wilder Nitro Line Deep Shadow around the key structural features. This was followed by chipping with Vallejo's German Black Highlight colour applied with a J's Work Chipping Effect sponge set. The same colour, thinned with water, was applied as vertical and lengthwise streaks and scrapes on the hull, the turret and the side skirts.

The model's wheels and tracks were finished to represent areas of wet and dry mud while they were still separate from the vehicle using Easy Mud's European Earth. The excess mud from the track pads was wiped away and the highlights treated with Rub 'n' Buff Silver. The wheels were also treated to a coat of Europen Earth, which was quickjly wiped off so that just a hint of dried mud remained. Wilder's Dark Wash was used on some of the wheels to represent wet mud or oil stains.

The tank's crew figures were painted using Tamiya Acrylics, Vallejo Model Colour paints and artist's oils. Details such as shoulder straps, piping and insignia were then picked out with a fine brush.

Since 1961, when Tamiya and Airfix both released their first plastic models of the Panther, in 1/35 and 1/76 scale respectively, this deservedly famous tank has been a favourite with modellers.

Other manufacturers were quick to market their own versions, in a number of scales, and although these early kits could be generously described as basic, they were affordable and easily obtained. The Tamiya model has long since been superseded by more detailed and accurate representations, but the Airfix kit is still available, attesting to its popularity at least. Encouragingly, the company has recently announced the release of a 1/35 scale Panther ausf G.

The last few decades have seen a boom in the plastic model industry and kits of the Panther are currently available in sizes ranging from 1/285 scale wargames tanks to massive 1/6 scale radio-controlled vehicles. As a consequence there are far too many to list here individually and, as with the other books in this series, I have chosen to concentrate on the most popular modelling scales of 1/35 and 1/48.

Similarly, as many of the currently available kits and accessories are covered in detail in *Panther Tanks: German Army and Waffen-SS Normandy Campaign, 1944, Panther Tanks: German Army Panzer Brigades Western and Eastern Fronts, 1944-1945* and *Panther Medium Tank: IV.SS-Panzerkorps Eastern Front, 1944* I have chosen to expand the Model Showcase section of this book and reduce the number of pages that would normally make up this chapter. Finally, the reader should note that on the following pages I have used the word Type in place of the more correct Ausführung, as at least one major manufacturer does, solely to avoid confusion. An index of manufacturers, with their contact details, can be found on page 64.

DRAGON MODELS LIMITED

Dragon Models was one of the first of the major manufacturers to offer accurate replicas in 1/35 scale and their kits are today something of a benchmark. The company's small scale releases are some of the best available. At the time of writing this Hong Kong-based company offered seven construction kits in both 1/35 and 1/72 scale representing variants of the Panther tanks in service at the time of the Italian campaign including a Type D, a Type A and an early Type G, all with Zimmerit texture. Also produced in 1/35 scale is a later Type G which could represent one of the tanks allocated to Panzer-Regiment 26. The smaller scale kit of the early Type G includes a number of well detailed and anatomically correct crew figures. In addition to these, Dragon produces a pre-painted early Type G in 1/72 scale although the model lacks Zimmerit, which was a standard feature in the summer of 1944, and is finished in markings that are somewhat dubious and not at all suitable for Italy. Dragon Models has also released a late production Panther Type A kit in 1/72 scale which would be entirely appropriate for the period covered by this book.

At left: Dragon Models' 1/35 scale kits suitable for the units mentioned in this book. The company also offers an early Panther Type A.

At right: The late model 1/35 scale Panther Type A kit built with the photo-etched brass and aluminium accessory set from Eduard Model Accessories.

TAMIYA INC

This Japanese company is currently the largest producer of scale model kits in the world, having begun life as a sawmill and timber supply firm. In 1959, after some success with wooden models, the company switched to injection moulded plastic and in 1961 released its first armoured vehicle kit, a motorised Panther.

By the early 1970s Tamiya was producing a large range of armoured vehicles, with complementary figures and accessories, and was almost solely responsible for the rise in popularity of 1/35 scale. Although rather basic by today's standards, these kits were highly accurate and detailed when compared to what else was available at the time. Importantly, they were all made to the same scale, encouraging modellers to build a collection, and affordable. The company's near monopoly of the 1/35 scale market remained unchallenged until the release of the first Dragon Models kits in 1987. The current catalogue lists a Type A, which is an older kit lacking some detail and features of the newer releases, an early Type G, in both a static and motorised version, and an early Type G with photo-etched Zimmerit texture. In 2003 Tamiya began releasing a series of models in 1/48 scale and this line has been extremely successful for the company, combining the potential for a high level of detail without the expense of the bigger kits.

The sole 1/48 scale offering at the time of writing is a later Type G which lacks the Zimmerit texture common to many of the tanks allocated to Panzer Regiment 4. Tamiya also produces radio-controlled models of a Type G in both 1/35 and 1/16 scale.

Below, right: Tamiya's large 1/25 scale Panther Type G. At left: Zimmerit texture in 1/35 scale sold separately and workable track, also in 1/35 scale. Note that the latter are the early variety without Stolen, or cleats.

RYE FIELD MODELS

Based in Hong Kong, this company released its first armour models, three highly accurate and detailed kits depicting Tiger I variants, within the short space of six months from late 2015. Rye Field Models also offers a Panther Type D and a Panther Type G, the latter being a very recent release. Both can be built as early or late production vehicles and the Panther Type G contains over 1,500 plastic parts, 196 photo-etched parts and 190 individual track links and track pins. The kit also contains a number of optional clear plastic parts to allow the detailed interior to be viewed. Shortly after the release of this model a less detailed version was marketed at a considerably reduced price. It seems strange that some kind of Zimmerit coating is not included with either model although the marking options allow for a vehicle in service during the summer of 1944.

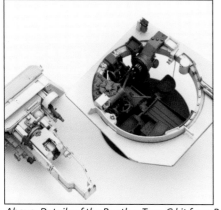  

Above: Details of the Panther Type G kit from Rye Field Models with full interior option. This model can be built as an early or later production vehicle.

TRUMPETER/HOBBY BOSS

Often thought to be separate entities, these Chinese companies are in fact owned by the same corporation, are located at the same address and are essentially the same firm although different models are marketed separately under the two labels. Hobby Boss produces a 1/16 scale early production Panther Type G, which actually depicts a tank assembled in September or October 1944, and a Panther Type A with Zimmerit in 1/35 scale. The company also offers a 1/35 scale Bergepanther model which utilises the hull and suspension of the Panther Type A kit.

At right: The 1/35 scale Panther Type A from Hobby Boss. This kit has an operational suspension and can be built with the drum-type commander's cupola suitable for the Type D.

Below: Details of the Trumpeter 1/16 scale Panther Type G model built as a Befehlspanzerwagen command tank.

MENG-MODEL

Founded in 2011, this Chinese company largely specialises in modern armour but also produces a number of Second World War subjects including a Panther Type A and Panther Type D, the latter with and without Zimmerit. The box of the Panther Type D also carries the logo of the Bovington Tank Museum, implying their cooperation, although I have been unable to confirm this. I should mention that a visit to the company's website, as with many Chinese model manufacturers, can be an exercise in frustration with the products listed here under the names of various dinosaurs.

Above: Meng-Model's 1/35 scale Panther Type A kit. The built and painted model represents a Panther Type A assembled after September 1943 and uses the optional Zimmerit which is included with the kit as thin plastic sheets.

ITALERI

This Italian company has been producing plastic models since its foundation in 1962. At present the catalogue contains a later model Panther Type G, a Panther Type D and a Panther Type A in 1/35 scale. In 1/72 scale Italeri produces a Panther Type G in their Fast Assembly range, the kit containing two models comprising just ten pieces each. The old ESCI Panther Type A kit in 1/72 scale, which Italeri produced for some time, is no long featured in the company's catalogue. Alone among the large model manufacturers Italeri has ventured into 1/56 scale with a Panther Type A kit. This scale complements 28mm wargames figures of which there are now quite a number on the market.

Italeri's 1/56 scale Panther Type A. The images below all show details from the 1/35 scale Panther ausf G kit.

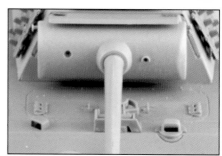

REVELL AND AIRFIX

No list of scale model Panther tanks would be complete without at least some mention of Airfix. The company's 1/76 scale Panther, a Type G model, was first released in 1961 and although the box art may have been altered over the years, the kit itself remains unchanged. Like Airfix, Revell has gone through many changes of ownership over the years since its founding, at one time operating as two distinct entities in the USA and Germany. The company's current catalogue shows the 1/72 Panther Type G and Panther Type A shown here at 1 and 2. Although these are both good kits, readers should be aware that the commander's cupola should have seven periscopes and not six, an inexplicable error in otherwise accurate models. The 1/35 scale Panther Type D (3) is a re-boxing of the ICM kit. Our example has been completed with the upgrade set from Voyager Model.

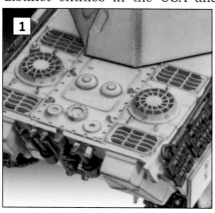
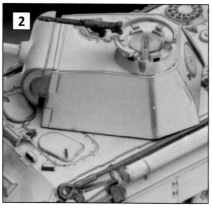

TAKOM

This is one of the newest model manufacturers, setting up shop in Hong Kong in 2013 as Takom World and shortly afterwards expanding to open a plant in mainland China where the models are actually produced. Most kits are in 1/35 scale and the company offers models of the early, mid and late production versions of the Panther Type A and Panther Type D versions, both with and without Zimmerit. All these models have detailed interiors and come with optional transparent parts for the hull and turret. Takom also produces two Bergepanther kits in 1/35 scale.

Above: The completely assembled hull and suspension of Takom's 1/35 scale Panther Type A model with full interior and, inset, detail shots of the turret interior and main gun breech. This model has also been released as a much less expensive version without the interior parts.

E.T. MODEL

E.T. Model, a relatively new manufacturer from China, produces upgrade sets in 1/72 and 1/35 scale in brass and resin. The company's current cattalogue includes etched-brass sets to fit the Dragon 1/35 scale Panther Type D, a 1/35 scale set for the recently released Tamiya Panther Type D, and a highly comprehensive set in photo-etched brass for the Dragon Models' early Panther Type G in 1/72 scale. Most sets are specifically designed, according to the company, to fit Dragon or Tamiya kits but some, for example the stowage bin, are referred to as universal.

Below: The E.T. Model upgrade set applied to the Dragon 1/72 scale Panther Type G.

Above, left: Parts from the 1/35 scale detail set for the Panther Type A and below that the Panther Type D.

EDUARD MODEL ACCESSORIES

Founded in 1989, this Czech company produces high quality upgrade kits in photo-etched metal and resin and a number of scale models. Currently available are extensive 1/35 scale detail sets to update the Tamiya Panther, including sets of Zimmerit produced in the patterns typical of MAN and MNH-manufactured vehicles, and both the Zvezda and Dragon Models Type G and late Type A. The company also offers vinyl masks to aid with painting the roadwheels. At the time of writing all the 1/48 and 1/72 scale sets for the Panther had been discontinued. The recently-released Type G kit from Tamiya includes a photo-etched Zimmerit set from Eduard.

At left: Tamiya's 1/48 scale Panther Type G built with the extensive Eduard photo-etched brass set which includes the MAN pattern Zimmerit coating.

Below: Dragon Models' 1/35 scale Panther Type G built with Eduard Model Accessories photo-etched brass set. Of note are the very fine buckles and clasps of the tools and the accurate brackets holding the hull Schürzen.

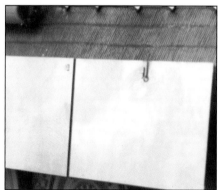

MODEL ARTISAN MORI

This small Japanese company produces resin upgrade parts for 1/35 scale armour models including detailed commander's cupolas and stowage boxes for the infrared sight equipment for the Panther. They also produce more general items such as crew uniforms and tool sets, including fire extinguishers, tow shackles and bolt cutters. Shown below, are: 1. The Panther drive sprocket with a selection of hub caps. 2. The early cast armoured exhaust covers. 3. The gun mantlet.

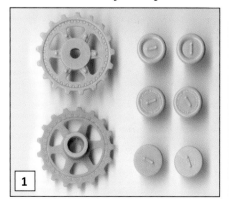
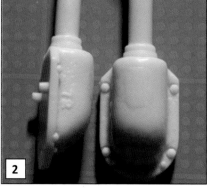
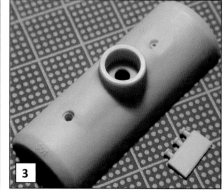

VOYAGER MODEL

Voyager Model, based in Shanghai, have been manufacturing upgrade sets for scale models since 2003 with the release of their first set for 1/35 scale armour. The company produces a number of items in both 1/72 and 1/35 scale in photo-etched brass and also resin, including wheel hubs, damaged road wheels, ammunition crates and boxes and fuel containers. In addition Voyager also offers highly detailed and accurate milled aluminium and brass barrels and muzzle brakes. Although most of these details would be compatible with almost all manufacturers' models, some sets are marketed as appropriate for the specific kits from Tamiya, Dragon, Zvezda and ICM.

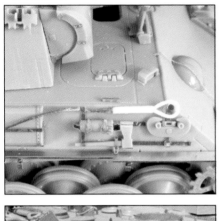

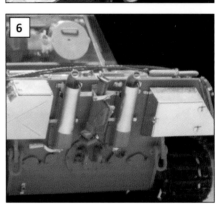

Above: Details of a number of 1/35 scale photo-etched brass upgrade sets from Voyager Model. 1. Tamiya Type G early production model showing the tool rack, jack block and towing coupling. 2. Dragon Models Type A later production showing the tube for the gun cleaning rods. 3. Dragon Type A later production. This image gives some idea of the large number of parts included in these sets. 4. Takom Type G showing the functioning stowage box lids. 5. Generic Schürzen and fender set for the Panther Type G. 6. Rye Field Models' Type G kit built with extra details from Voyager. I should mention that this configuration, with a standard stowage box and special container for the infrared sighting equipment, would not have been encountered on the Italian Front.

ROYAL MODEL

Founded in the early 1990s, this Italian company produces high-quality accessories and aftermarket parts in metal and resin. The catalogue includes complete upgrade sets for both the Dragon early and late Type A, the Tamiya Type G and the Italeri Type A, all in 1/35 scale. Royal Model also offers photo-etched brass hull Schürzen for the Type A and G which are appropriate for all 1/35 scale kits. Other 1/35 scale items include two interior detail sets for the Type A and photo-etched Zimmerit for the Type A, either factory fresh or damaged. More generic parts in resin and brass are an engine transmission, detailed rear stowage bins, engine grills and a Kugelblende machine-gun mount.

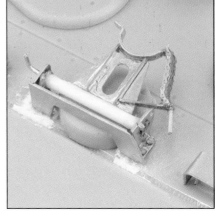

Above, from left to right: Examples of the very high standard of detail incorporated into Royal Model's 1/35 scale upgrade sets. Shown here are the tool bracket for the hull left-hand side, the locking mechanism of the commander's cupola hatch in the open position and the gun travel lock for a Panther Type A or Type D.

ROCHM MODEL

This company is owned and managed by master modeller Sheng Hui whose work has appeared in a number of books in the TankCraft series. Initially specialising in 1/35 scale detail sets in resin, photo-etched brass and aluminium for the Tiger I, the company moved onto the Tiger II series and then the Panther currently offering forty-five different upgrade sets as part of a program titled *Evolution of*

the Panther which is intended to continue into the very last production models. Primarily intended for the Meng, Dragon and Zvezda models, many of the parts would of course be suitable for most 1/35 scale kits. ROCHM Model's products offer exceptional detail and considering the quality, are reasonably priced. Detail sets in 1/48 and 1/72 scale are currently in the planning stage.

Above: Dragon Model's 1/35 scale Panther Type A built and painted by Sheng Hui using details from his photo-etched range. Below: A selection of resin and photo-etched brass details including tool clamps, a fire extinguisher and gun cleaning rod housing for early and mid-production Panther Type A tanks in 1/35 scale.

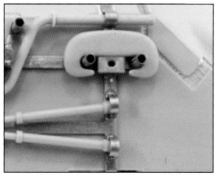

ABER

For some time now Tamiya has included a number of Aber products with their models. A full list of the accessories made specifically for the Panther in all scales would be far too large to reproduce on this page and the reader can find the company's contact

details on page 64. Shown below are: 1. Parts of the hull side fender and front mudguard set for a Panther Type G. 2. The tube used to house the gun cleaning rods for a Panther Type G. 3. The barrel for the hull MG 34. All items are in 1/35 scale.

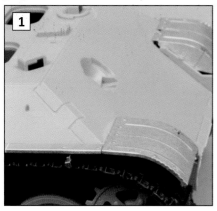
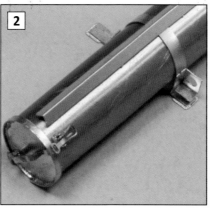
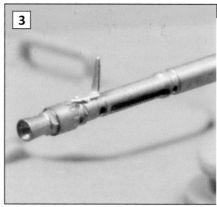

As I.Abteilung, Panzer-Regiment 4 was the only Panther unit to see combat in the Italian campaign this section focuses on the variants employed by that battalion. When I.Abteilung left Germany for the front in January 1944 the headquarters platoons and four Panzer companies contained seventy-six Pzkpfw V tanks and their distribution is shown in the organisational chart on page 62.

The three purpose-built Befehlswagen command tanks of the battalion headquarters were all Pzkpfw V ausf D vehicles fitted with the armoured cover for the FuG 8 radio antenna and insulator on the engine deck and the rack for the antenna extensions under the tube for the gun cleaning rods on the hull right side. These features are shown in the drawings and photographs throughout this book. These vehicles are usually assumed to have been assembled prior to September 1943 when the application of Zimmerit anti-magnetic mine paste was introduced into production but a series of photographs, which unfortunately cannot be reproduced here, show that at least one had a factory-applied coat of the paste. This tank is shown on page 18 of the Camouflage & Markings section. The remaining seventy-three tanks were, for the most part, Pzkpfw V ausf A models but photographs exist of Pzkpfw V ausf D tanks which are clearly not command vehicles. Unfortunately, in each instance, these tanks have been damaged and abandoned and none carry company numbers although they must be from Panzer-Regiment 4. The battalion's Pzkpfw V ausf A tanks were a mix of earlier production models, with the twin apertures for the binocular TZF 12 gun sight and the so-called letterbox opening for the MG 34 in the hull glacis, and vehicles assembled after November 1943 as evidenced the single aperture in the gun mantlet for the monocular TZF 12a sight and the distinctive Kugelblende machine-gun mounting. All were coated with Zimmerit and the differences achieved in the texture of the paste during its application is discussed on page 60. A total of thirty-eight new tanks were shipped to the battalion in May and June 1944 and these deliveries probably contained the first examples of the Pzkpfw V ausf G. Again, all these tanks would have been coated with Zimmerit. The replacement tanks allocated in September and October 1944 probably consisted in the main of Pzkpfw V ausf G models and photographs show that the later arrivals did not have Zimmerit.

The Pzkpfw V ausf A was manufactured by the firms of Maschinenfabrik Augsburg-Nürnberg AG (MAN), Daimler-Benz, Maschinenfabrik Niedersachsen Hanover (MNH) and Deutsche Maschinenbau-Aktiengesellschaft (DEMAG) with production beginning in August 1943 and ending in July 1944. When the Panther II project was postponed, and eventually abandoned, many of its simplified design aspects were incorporated into the chassis of the Pzkpfw V ausf G and production began in March 1944. All the commercial firms mentioned above were involved in the manufacture of the new version except DEMAG which switched to production of the Bergepanther recovery tank. Listed below are the major modifications that were instituted from the commencement of the Pzkpfw V ausf A production run in August 1943 to October 1944 when the last examples of the Pzkpfw V ausf G reached the battalion. As relatively few Pzkpfw V ausf D tanks were on hand I have mentioned these only briefly and the production features of this tank, and indeed its development, are examined in some detail in *TankCraft 34: Panther Medium Tank German Army and Waffen-SS, Eastern Front Summer 1943.*

August 1943. The first Panther ausf A models leave the assembly plants. Just three examples of the new variant are completed in this month, all by the MNH plant at Hannover. In the same month, operational units are ordered to replace the 16-bolt road wheels with the newer 24-bolt versions. Since the previous June, the 16-bolt wheels had been reinforced with large rivets placed between each bolt. The 24-bolt road wheels were introduced into production gradually and were at first only fitted to the second position with the 16-bolt versions being used until stocks were exhausted. The Heereswaffenamt (HWA) orders that a ring for an anti-aircraft machine gun be fitted to the cupola of Panther ausf D model. However, an armaments ministry report of 24 August complains that none of the vehicles from that month's production run feature this modification.

September 1943. Tracks with six Stollen, or chevrons, cast into the face of each link are incorporated into production. The manufacturers are ordered to apply a coat of Zimmerit anti-magnetic mine paste to all vehicles as part of the assembly process. The exact date that this order was put into effect is unknown and photographs exist of vehicles completed at

the beginning of October that do not have Zimmerit, suggesting that some firms at least may have had difficulty obtaining sufficient quantities of the paste. Production of the Panther ausf D ends and given that just thirty-seven vehicles are assembled in this month, very few examples of this model would have received a coat of Zimmerit at the assembly plants.

November 1943. A ball mount for the hull machine gun, the Kugelblende, is incorporated into production replacing the so-called letterbox opening (1). As the new mount contains a sight for the machine gun it is felt that the radio operator's forward facing periscope is now superfluous and it is no longer fitted. The binocular TZF.12 gun sight is replaced by the monocular TZF.12a version. Until supplies of single aperture gun mantlets are available the second, outer sight aperture is sealed with an armoured plug although these vehicles retained the wider rain channel. A number of tanks produced in November and December are fitted with a towing coupling bolted onto the hull rear plate along the lower edge below the engine access hatch. This is identical to the coupling fitted to the Bergepanther recovery vehicle. As this interfered with

Notes

1. It was at one time accepted that the Kugelblende mounting was an identifying feature of the Pzkpfw V ausf A but as many as 600 tanks were manufactured without this modification and the hulls were essentially unchanged from the Panther ausf D.

............text continued on page 52

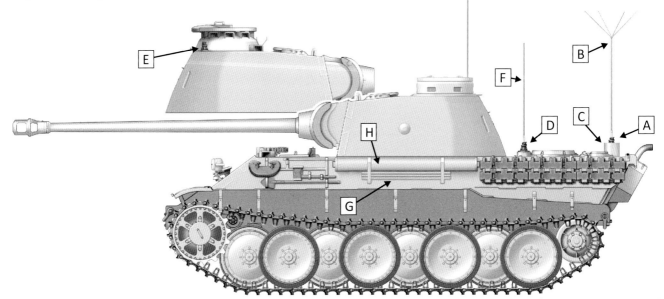

Above: Pzkpfw V Panther ausf D produced prior to September 1943. The most distinctive feature of this model was the simple, cylindrical commander's cupola (A) which from August 1943 was fitted with a ring mount (B) to accommodate the bracket for an anti-aircraft machine gun. The dove-tailed join of the turret front and side plates (C) was also noticeably different to the square edges of the Pzkpfw V ausf A turret. Note that this vehicle has two road wheels (D) strengthened by the addition of sixteen rivets, a practice that was introduced between June and August 1943. These rivets were of roughly the same size as the bolts and are difficult to differentiate in contemporary photographs. In August, new 24-bolt roadwheels were incorporated into the assembly process which were intended to replace the 16-bolt variants (E) completely but never did. The turret pistol port (F) was retained with production of the Pzkpfw V ausf A until December 1943. The supports for the hull Schürzen (G) were fixed into brackets welded to the underside of the hull panniers. Note the single Bosch headlight (H) mounted on the left-hand side of the glacis above the fender.

Above: The Panzerbefehlswagen (PzBefWg) Panther Sdkfz 267 and Sdkfz 268 were purpose-built command vehicles and were based on all models of the Panther including the Pzkpfw V ausf D and Pzkpfw V ausf A versions shown here. The Sdkfz 268 is sometimes described as an air liaison vehicle and the difference between the two lay in the radio equipment installed in each. The Sdkfz 267 was fitted with a Funkgerät (FuG) 8 command radio which had a range of some 70 kilometres, although voice transmissions were usually limited to less than half that distance. The porcelain insulator (A) for the radio's 1.8-metre Sternantenne D (B) was mounted on the engine deck and protected by an armoured cylinder (C and 1 below). The insulator and 2.0-metre Stabantenne for the FuG 5 radio, which in normal production models was fitted in a mount on the hull left side (D and 2 below), was moved to a position on the turret roof to the right of the commander's cupola (E and 3 below). This radio provided tank-to-tank communication. On the Sdkfz 268 the FuG 5 antenna and its insulator were also mounted on the turret roof while its usual placed on the hull left side was taken by a 1.4-metre Stabantenne for an FuG 7 radio (F). The latter was matched to the Luftwaffe's FuG 17 transceiver and was supposed to be used for ground support operations. All the command versions were manufactured by MAN and all were wired to accept the three types of radio mentioned here and as most crews fitted all three antennas, whether they received a signal or not, the most obvious differences were internal. On most command vehicles, but not all, three tubes (G), fixed in a bracket under the gun-cleaning rod housing (H) on the left side of the hull, held the Steckmastrohre, or extension masts, which were used to increase the range of the FuG 8 transmitter.

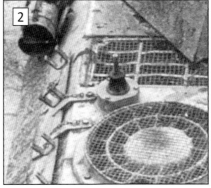

The initial allocations of Panther tanks to I.Abteilung, Panzer-Regiment 4, shipped by the Heereszeugamt in December 1943 and January 1944, were primarily made up of Pzkpfw V ausf A tanks. But a number of pre-September 1943 production Pzkpfw ausf D vehicles must have accompanied the battalion to Italy, other than the three Panzerbefehlswagen which are well documented, as shown by the photographs on this page. Above: This image is unfortunately undated but was probably made during the summer of 1944 when the battalion was fighting between Perugia and Arezzo. This tank is completely devoid of any Zimmerit and is fitted with the early 16-bolt road wheels, one of which is the reinforced version. It has the second pattern drive sprocket and TZF.12 binocular gun sight and just visible is the turret communications port which was dropped from production in August 1943. What may be the remains of a bracket on the hull side is too far towards the rear to have held the Steckmasten antenna extension rods, which would identify a Panzerbefehlswagen, and the coaxial machine gun is still in place. Below: Possibly photographed during the early autumn of 1944 this Panther ausf D does not have the turret communications port and is fitted with the cupola ring for the anti-aircraft machine gun suggesting that it was built after August 1943 but it does have other early features including the first pattern gun cleaning rod tube. Note the towing coupling very roughly attached to the engine access hatch. This at least dates the photograph to some time after April 1944. Note also that the main gun is missing and the aperture for the mantlet has a field-modified cover made from sheet metal.

.........................text continued from page 49

Notes

1. None of the Panther ausf A tanks allocated to I.Abteilung, Panzer-Regiment 4 before May 1944 would have been fitted with the Nahverteidigungswaffe.

ground clearance it is soon dropped from production and although the number of tanks actually fitted with the coupling was small, most Panther ausf A models manufactured up to April 1944 had the necessary brackets and holes, the latter sealed with four bolts. Units in the field are ordered to apply Zimmerit to those tanks which had not received a coat before leaving the factories.

December 1943. The small pistol ports, referred to as MP Stopfen, on either side of the turret are dropped from production. It was intended that these be replaced by the Nahverteidigungswaffe, or close defence weapon, which was to be mounted in the turret roof. This breech-loaded grenade launcher could be traversed through 360 degrees and was capable of firing smoke candles, grenades and flares from inside the turret. A hole was cut in the turret roof, to the right of the cupola, into which the Nahverteidigungswaffe was meant to be fitted but due to difficulties with supply

none were available until March 1944 and the turrets of many Panther ausf A models assembled in February and March are instead fitted with a circular plate covering the hole and held in place by four bolts (1).

January 1944. Changes to the crew compartment heater meant that the left side manifold was no longer fed cooling air and to compensate for this two cooling pipes are added to the engine exhaust manifold. It should be mentioned that these pipes were never fitted to the right side or as a single pipe and examples seen today in museums have been re-assembled incorrectly.

February 1944. A vertical mount for the 20-ton jack replaces the previous horizontal arrangement which held a 15-ton jack. Stocks of the latter are held in reserve and MAN is contracted to design a suitable vertical mount. Beginning in February, a towing coupling is welded directly to the engine access hatch on the

............text continued on page 55

At left: The six individual hull Schürzen plates were held in place by support arms which were fitted into small brackets welded to the underside of the hull panniers.

Above: A Pzkpfw V Panther ausf A tank produced after January 1944 when the turret side pistol ports were dropped from production. The new version was based on the Panther ausf D chassis with the most obvious change being the inclusion of a completely re-designed cast cupola (A and 1 below) for the tank's commander which featured seven periscopes each protected by an armoured cowling (B). In addition, a single periscope for the loader (C) was fitted into the turret roof behind the fume extractor (D and 2 below). The interlocking joints of the turret front and side plates were now squared off, whereas those of the Panther ausf D had been dovetailed, and the cast sides behind the gun mantlet were reshaped to accommodate a new type of seal. This tank is fitted with the 24-bolt road wheels (E) introduced from August 1943 and the Kugelblende machine-gun mount (F and 3 below) incorporated in November of the same year. All drawings are shown without Zimmerit for the sake of clarity.

Photographed during the late summer of 1944, this Panther ausf A is tank 103 of the battalion headquarters, also shown on page 14. This vehicle was assembled before November 1943 when the Kugelblende machine-gun mount was introduced and is coated in Zimmerit that has been textured in the pattern which is indicative of MAN-produced Panthers. Note that it is fitted with the early binocular gun sight and note also the field-modified stowage boxes on the hull engine deck which were a common feature of this battalion's tanks.

This Panther ausf A of 3.Kompanie, Panzer-Regiment 4 was disabled and abandoned near Ponte Corvo, west of Cassino, on 25 May 1944. The pattern of Zimmerit, made up of short strokes or ridges, identifies this as a DEMAG-built tank. Note the field-modified stowage boxes and the first type of towing coupling which was fitted to some tanks in November and December 1943. Another photograph of this tank can be seen on page 6 and it is also depicted in the Camouflage & Markings section on page 20.

Photographed near Aprilia after the battles around Anzio in early 1944, this early production Panther ausf A of 3.Kompanie has the so-called letterbox aperture for the MG 34 on the hull glacis and pistol port on the turret side. The Zimmerit has been applied in a pattern used by MAN and although difficult to see in this image, the vertical lines on the turret sides have been applied diagonally. This vehicle is also shown on page 19 of the Camouflage & Markings section.

...........................text continued from page 52

hull rear plate. This towing coupling is of a much simplified design when compared to the version that was fitted to some tanks in November 1943. Panthers assembled by MNH are fitted with the old access hatch without the coupling until mid-April 1944.

March 1944. The first production models of the Panther ausf G are completed. The most distinctive feature of the new model are the angled sides of the hull each made up from a single plate. The turret is initially the same as that used for the Panther ausf A with its cast cupola and would only differ in small details as production continued and the war progressed.

Other features which differentiate the Panther ausf G from the earlier models include new driver's and radio-operator's hatches which are now hinged, as opposed to the pivoting versions of the earlier tanks, while the single Bosch headlight is moved from the glacis to the left fender. In addition, the tool stowage on the hull sides is revised and this can be seen in the colour profiles of the Camouflage & Markings section of this book. Most of these features were taken from the design of the Panther II.

May 1944. To simplify construction, the cast armoured guards that protect the exhaust manifolds where they enter the hull are replaced by welded versions.

June 1944. Sheet metal covers are fitted over the exhaust pipes above the armoured guards of the Panther ausf G. These pipes regularly become hot enough to produce a visible glow, making the tank an easy target. In response to complaints from tank crews that the turret rear access hatch can not be opened from the outside, a handle is added. Three sockets, or Pilzen, are welded to the turret roof to accommodate the 2-ton Befehlskran jib boom. These last two modifications were also to be carried out by units in the field and incorporated into the assembly of the Panther ausf A, which was still in production.

July 1944. It was found that the periscopes fitted to the cast commander's cupola were liable to come loose if the tank experienced any violent vibration and, in addition, they were difficult to remove and replace.

In this month, a frame and improved fastener is installed. At the same time the assembly plants are ordered to cease the installation of a mount for an observation periscope, or Sehstab, in the cupola. Both these modifications were essentially internal and are rarely seen in photographs. On 17 July, the decision is taken to drop the air intake cover on the front hull from production but this is reversed within days. Production of the Panther ausf A ends (1).

Notes

1. The June and July vehicles were all assembled by MNH. MAN and Daimler-Benz had ceased production in March and May 1944 respectively. The last Panther ausf A built by DEMAG is thought to have left the factory in the previous January but reliable figures are not available for this company.

This Panther ausf G was probably one of the tanks allocated to I.Abteilung, Panzer-Regiment 4 in September 1944 by Nachschub Südwest. It has the sheet metal covers that were fitted to the exhaust pipes from June 1944 and, just visible on the turret roof, the Pilzen, or sockets, which accommodated the 2-ton Befehlskran jib boom and which were incorporated into production at the same time. This tank was captured intact by the British and used until the end of the war.

Notes

1. These patterns and the colours, and the schemes instituted in the following months, are discussed in some detail in *TankCraft 18: Panther Tanks German Army and Waffen-SS, Defence of the West 1945.*

August 1944. In line with an order issued in the previous month, a rain guard is fitted over the driver's periscope. A metal debris guard is added to the turret roof to cover the gap behind the mantlet of the main gun. The hatches of the driver and radio operator are fitted with new hinge fasteners which allow the hatches to be opened upward and jettisoned in an emergency. On 19 August the HWA orders that camouflage colours are to be applied at the assembly plants. A more or less standardised scheme is to consist of a base coat of Dunkelgelb 7028 over which large patches of Olivgrün RAL 6003 and Rotbraun RAL 8017 are to be painted (1). Every effort is to be made to deliver the remaining consignment in the new scheme and given that 356 vehicles are completed in this month as many as one third may have received the new camouflage.

September 1944. The application of Zimmerit ceases and from 9 September most, if not all, tanks leave the assembly plants without a coat of the anti-magnetic mine paste. Interior surfaces are no longer to be painted with Elfenbein RAL 1001 but instead left in their primer coat. A new gun mantlet, which features a prominent lower chin, or Kinnblende, is incorporated into production. Introduction of this new mantlet was extremely slow and the earlier round design was used until the end of the war. In all the photographs I have been able to examine of Panther ausf G tanks serving in Italy I have been unable to find a single example. A lengthened rain guard was fitted over the sight aperture of the gun mantlet. A small number of vehicles are fitted with FG 1250 infrared searchlights and sighting equipment. A limited number of MAN produced vehicles, perhaps as few as twenty-four, are fitted with steel-tyred road wheels. Again, none of these seem to have found there way to Italy.

October 1944. A self-cleaning rear idler replaces the version that had been used since production commenced. An improved crew internal compartment heater, or Kampfraumheizung, is introduced. The distinctive housing for the heater's cooling fan, situated on the rear deck, is clearly visible in period photographs. Three mounts to hold poison gas identification panels are fitted to the turret roof. In an effort to further reduce the glow produced by the exhaust pipes, instructions are issued that both are to be fitted with Flammenvernichter mufflers but it is possible that this modification was not actually fitted until December.

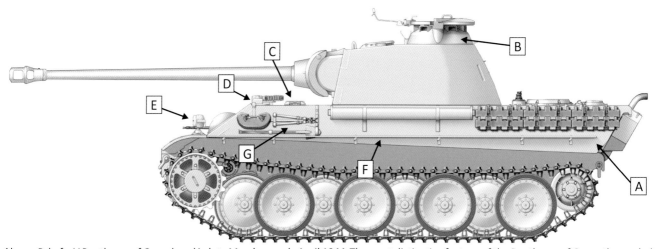

Above: Pzkpfw V Panther ausf G produced in late March or early April 1944. The most distinctive feature of the Panther ausf G was the angled sides of the redesigned hull, fabricated from single plates (A and 1 below). The turret was initially the same as the Panther ausf A with its cast cupola (B) and only differed in small details as production continued. Other new features included the driver's and radio-operator's hatches (C and 2 below), which were now hinged as opposed to the pivoting versions, and the deletion of the prominent driver's visor. In place of the latter a periscope (D and 3 below) with an armoured cover was installed on the hull roof in front of the driver's hatch. The single Bosch headlight (E) was moved from the glacis to the left fender. The hull Schürzen, or armoured skirts, were now fixed to an extended track guard (F) which was fixed to the hull sides. In addition, the tool stowage on the hull sides was revised (G). The rear deck was completely redesigned including the louvres and the air intakes.

One particular modification deserves special mention. On 18 December 1944 the Heereswaffenamt ordered that units in the field were to fabricate steel covers to protect the air intake and exhaust louvres on the Panther tank's rear deck from aircraft attack or splinters from artillery shells. Detailed drawings and photographs accompanied the order and it was specified that the covers be made from hull Schürzen plates. The available evidence shows that this modification was carried out on most, but not all, the Panthers of I.Abteilung, Panzer-Regiment 4, probably during the enforced hiatus of the winter of 1944-1945. In addition to the hull armour, the battalion's workshops were able to develop armoured protection for the turret roof in the shape of spaced metal plates and, as far as is know, the only Panthers fitted with this modification were those serving on the Italian Front. It should be mentioned that the concept of additional armour protection for the turret roof was not new and had been employed from late 1943 by Panzer-Regiment 21 while that unit's Pzkpfw IV tanks were serving on the Russian Front.

At left: This photograph was included with the 18 December 1944 order and showed in detail how the protective plates for the rear engine deck were to be fabricated. The cover for the cooling air exhaust fan could be pivoted upwards by removing the bolt marked here as 11. Below: A plan view of the turret armour added to the tanks of I.Abteilung, Panzer-Regiment 4. Photographs show that the design was consistent throughout the battalion with the large hole cut for the Nahverteidigungswaffe close-defence weapon.

Below: Photographed during the early summer of 1945, this MAN-built Panther ausf G is fitted with turret roof armour. Although the official order stipulated that hull Schürzen plates were to be used in the construction of the engine deck armour the front section of the turret armour is much wider than a single plate. Other photographs of this tank show that it was not fitted with the hull armour plates.

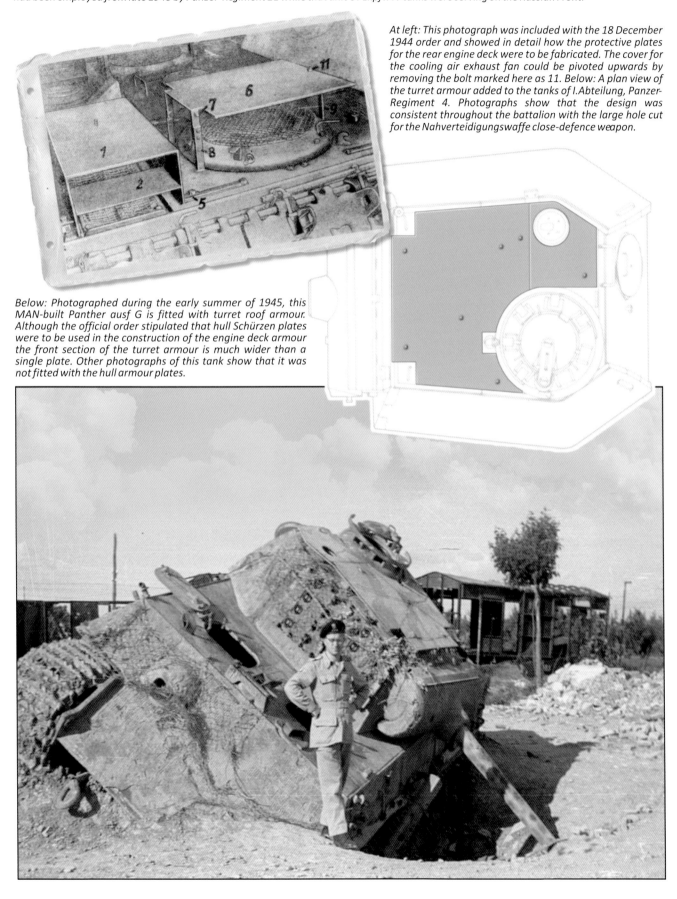

Photographed near the village of Sesto Imolese, east of Bologna, on 13 April 1945, this Panther ausf A was built after November 1943 when the Kugelblende machine-gun mount was introduced. The field-modified turret roof and engine deck armour are still intact although almost all the Zimmerit has either broken away or been burnt off. This vehicle was photographed from several angles and the images seem to show that additional armour plates have also been fitted to the turret sides. This tank is also shown on page 25.

This Panther ausf G of 4.Kompanie, Panzer-Regiment 26 was disabled in a night action on 15 April 1945 and was almost certainly one of the tanks allocated to the battalion in September and October 1944. The field-modified engine deck armour is visible here and other photographs in this series show the turret roof armour. This tank is also shown and discussed on page 26 of the Camouflage & Markings section.

The purpose and application of Zimmerit has been examined in earlier books in the TankCraft series, including those which covered the Pzkpfw V Panther, but as the paste would have been applied to most of the tanks deployed to Italy the picture would not be complete without some explanation being offered here. Additionally, the method of application, which left a distinctive texture, could identify a specific manufacturer and this often helps with explaining or identifying other modifications.

As many readers will know, German infantry units had been equipped with a number of magnetic anti-tank grenades, collectively known as Hafthohlladung, from late 1942. But the widely accepted narrative that the adoption of Zimmerit into the tank assembly process was an effort to pre-empt the possible introduction of similar weapons by the Western Allies and the Soviets is now open to question. British intelligence reports released since the end of the war indicate that some kind of magnetic mine was already in service with the Red Army and that the development of both the Hafthohlladung and Zimmerit were reactions to a threat that had already materialised.

The engineers at Henschel und Sohn, the company which manufactured the Tiger and also produced 130 examples of the Pzkpfw V ausf D, were tasked with finding some kind of thick cement which could be applied to the surfaces of an armoured vehicle in the expectation that this coating would neutralise the magnetic properties of the mines and render them useless. Herr Robert Pertuss, the chief engineer at Henschel, stated that a quick-drying compound marketed as Nitro-Spachtel was obtained from I. G. Farbenindustrie and initially applied as an experiment to a single Tiger I (1).

It was found that the cement dried and could be painted after only three hours although this time could be reduced by the use of a blowtorch. This process was considerably less complicated than that required for the commercially-available Zimmerite, as we shall see (2).

In August 1945, the production director and engineers at Henschel, including Herr Pertuss, were interrogated by British intelligence officers and stated that the cement applied to their tanks, which they referred to as Zimmerit, was obtained from Chemische Werke Zimmer AG of Berlin although they assumed that other companies were involved in production as such large quantities were required.

The managers at I. G. Farbenindustrie were also questioned at about the same time and could offer no information about Zimmerit but said that they knew of Chemische Werke Zimmer AG as quantities of Polyvinyl Acetate had been sold to the Berlin company. It shoud be borne in mind that the properties of the paste, which has come to characterise German tanks of the 1944 battles, was probably of little concern to the engineers who designed those tanks. Herr Pertuss in particular was quite offended when he was questioned for hours about Zimmerit

while the technical advances made by the Henschel engineers and designers were largely ignored (3). What is interesting about this account is that the use of the terms Nitro-Spachtel and Zimmerit by the same sources raises the possibility that more than one commercially-available compound was used to give tanks of this period their distinctive textured appearance. The word Zimmerit may have come to be used generically to describe a range of products.

Marketed as Zimmerite, but often spelled as Zimmerit, the thick putty-like paste was tested by the British and found to be made up mainly of Barium Sulphate and Polyvinyl Acetate with the addition of an ochre pigment and Zinc Sulphide. The reaction of Barium Sulphate with Zinc Sulphide tends to produce a white colour which would have lightened the ochre pigment somewhat. As a binding agent, ordinary sawdust was added. The firm of Chemische Werke Zimmer AG specialised in the manufacture of sealing compounds for large construction projects. As delivered, the paste contained a volatile solvent which smelled of acetone which was burnt off during the application process.

The paste was to be applied to all the vertical and sloped surfaces of tanks and assault guns, including the hull sides behind the wheels, to the height that an average man could reach, before the vehicles left the assembly plants. Moving parts and detachable items, such as hinges and tools, were not to be coated as it was expected that the paste would be quickly worn away. Officially, Zimmerit was not to be applied to either hull or turret Schürzen although photographic evidence shows that this order was frequently ignored.

The application itself was quite complicated and required two coats and each coat needed to be left to cure for at least four hours. Once dry the paste became quite hard and it was then heat-treated with a blowtorch and, with special tools, fashioned into a pattern of ridges. It was the resulting ridges which denied the magnets the flat surface they needed, the paste itself having no inherent anti-magnetic properties. The use of the blowtorch had to be undertaken with special care as the Polyvinyl Acetate contained Benzine. The process of drying and curing could take from three to six days depending on the atmospheric conditions. Compare this process to the application of Nitro-Spachtel mentioned earlier.

Notes

1. This product, marketed under the same name, is still being manufactured today. It is largely used in the automotive repair industry.

2. Interestingly, Herr Pertuss implied that Nitro-Spachtel was used in the assembly of the Tiger until the end of production.

3 The British, for their part, were convinced that Zimmerit was some kind of advanced camouflage.

Notes

1. A Panzerbefehlswagen V ausf D known to have been photographed in Italy was coated in Zimmerit in the pattern most often associated with MAN Panther ausf A tanks and is shown on page 18 of the Camouflage & Markings section. For copyright reasons I cannot reproduce the series of photographs here.

The specification calling for the application of Zimmerit was issued to the assembly plants in August 1943 and the first tanks probably received a coat of the paste in the following September at the MAN assembly plant. Panther ausf A vehicles known to have been built in late September 1943 by MNH can be seen in photographs without a coating of Zimmerit and tanks which left the Daimler-Benz factory as late as the first week of October do not have the paste and it is likely that the company did not acquire stocks of Zimmerit until the end of the month.

Production of the Panther ausf D ended in September and as just thirty-seven tanks left the factories in that same month it is unlikely that many received a coat at the assembly plants. Indeed, at least one authoritative sources contends that no Panther ausf D was coated with Zimmerit before leaving the factories. But it should be remembered that Henschel und Sohn

had experimented with an alternative which was indistinguishable and the possibility that this was used on at least some of the company's September production run of ten tanks cannot be discounted (1).

The first examples of the Panther ausf G were completed in March and April 1944 and it is likely that the allocation of twenty tanks shipped from Nachschub Südwest to I.Abteilung, Panzer-Regiment 4 in the following September contained a number of this model, probably coated in Zimmerit.

Each company created special tools to complete the application of Zimmerit and the resulting pattern of ridges or grids can identify the manufacturer of a particular tank. It should be mentioned that these conclusions have been arrived at largely by the examination of photographic evidence and should at best be regarded as a general rule to which possible exceptions exist.

Daimler-Benz Panther ausf A. This pattern was characterised by a rather flat application which was afterwards roughened with short strokes often, but not always, made on the diagonal. The surface was then broken up by vertical and horizontal lines which formed a grid which could also be very roughly applied, the lines often straying off course. The grid also varied considerably in size but did not extend to the cupola. With the exception of the initial rough application, this pattern can be very similar to that seen on Panther tanks produced by MNH and the two are often difficult, if not impossible, to differentiate in photographs. Both the images reproduced above show Panther ausf A tanks.

Daimler-Benz Panther ausf G. The pattern used on the earlier version was maintained with the grid varying in size from quite large, as also seen on the MNH Panther ausf G models, to the so-called 'small square' version applied to the Jagdpanthers built by MIAG. However, a grid of approximately 10 centimetre squares is most commonly seen in photographs. There is some evidence that Daimler-Benz adopted this pattern, identified by its roughened finish, solely to distinguish their Panthers from those produced by the company's main rival, MAN.

DEMAG Panther ausf A. This pattern was made up of short horizontal strokes, probably applied with a trowel, which were then separated by deep vertical lines. Some vehicles also featured horizontal lines which then formed a grid and this has led to the DEMAG patterns being incorrectly assumed to be a version of the MAN Zimmerit. The company assembled just fifty Panther ausf A tanks before production swithed to the Bergepanther recovery vehicle.

MAN Panther ausf A. The Zimmerit coating was typically made up of short vertical strokes applied with a roller and was characterised by a very orderly appearance. Over the short strokes or ridges, vertical and horizontal lines forming a grid of about 10 centimetres square were worked into the paste with a pallet knife or trowel. These longer lines were less orderly but consistent with the same number seen on different vehicles. Diagonal lines are frequently encountered with vehicles assembled after October and this may be due to the practice of the turret manufacturers applying Zimmerit before the turret was delivered to the assembly plant. The September and October production vehicles, perhaps as many as 100, had Zimmerit patterns made up of horizontal strokes as applied to the Tiger I. Shown above is a Panzerbefehlswagen V ausf A at left with a Panther ausf G at right. Note that the Zimmerit applied to the command tank does not have the vertical line that would create a grid.

MAN Panther ausf G. The pattern that had been applied to the Panther ausf A models was maintained but in a more uniform manner with different vehicles displaying the same number of lines on turret sides, hull fronts and other surfaces. Diagonal lines are rarely seen. Another similar pattern was used, employing a slightly larger roller which left a thicker coat of Zimmerit and necessitated a grid of about 15 centimetres square. That this pattern does not seem to have been applied to surfaces such as mudguards may suggest that it was a later version. It seems that Zimmerit was not applied to the commander's cupola on any MAN variants.

MNH Panther ausf A. The coating applied to Panther ausf A models featured a flat, rather smooth application broken up by deeply scored vertical and horizontal lines which formed a grid. As a general rule Zimmerit was applied to the fenders but not the stowage bins which were left untreated on some vehicles. Although rare, there are instances of this pattern being extended to the commander's cupola. An example is shown above at left.

MNH Panther ausf G. In July 1944, MNH switched to production of the Panther ausf G and the pattern was changed to one made up of deep horizontal strokes applied with a trowel, often referred to today as the 'ladder pattern'. Over this, an orderly grid of approximately 10 centimetres square was inscribed with a trowel or similar tool. Zimmerit was applied to the commander's cupola. This process could only have been in use for just over nine weeks and photographic examples are quite rare. In addition, the turrets of the very first Panther ausf G tanks assembled by MNH featured the texture seen on the firm's Panther ausf A vehicles while the hull was finished with the new pattern. Tanks produced by this firm were still being completed with Zimmerit on 14 September 1944, a full week after the official decision had been taken to discontinue its use. An example is shown above at right.

Many photographs exist of tanks coated in patterns which do not conform to those listed above and it is common to read of field-applied Zimmerit as a means of explaining the many anomalies. However, when one considers how complicated the process of covering a complete armoured vehicle was, requiring 160 kilograms of paste for a single Panther, with long waiting periods between each step and the use of a blowtorch with what was essentially a flammable compound, it seems likely that older or damaged tanks received their coating of Zimmerit when they were withdrawn from the front for repairs at larger workshops far in the rear.

I.ABTEILUNG, PANZER-REGIMENT 4, JANUARY 1944

All formations of the German Army were organised according to detailed tables of establishment referred to as Kriegstärkenachweisung (KstN) which showed the official composition of a unit, listing the exact number of personnel and type of equipment from vehicles to small arms. The tables were numbered and dated, the latter being all-important as some numbers were often duplicated. The KstN were accompanied by Kriegsausrüstungsnachweisung (KAN) which listed minor items in detail such as tools and fuel containers but these need not concern us here. A directive of 5 May 1943 ordered that III.Abteilung, Panzer-Regiment 4 be organised in accordance with the KstN being employed at that time by units converting to the Panther. But on 19 October 1943 a new order was issued renaming the battalion as I.Abteilung and advising that amended KstN, all annotated as Gemischtes, or mixed, were to be used and these are shown below. As mentioned in the main text, the battalion was accompanied to Italy by the headquarters of Panzer-Regiment 69 which had been assigned the five Pzkpfw IV ausf H shown here in December 1944. The three Panzerbefehlswagen V command tanks are assumed on basis of I.Abteilung, Panzer-Regiment 4 receiving seventy-nine tanks in total, as opposed to the authorised seventy-six, and a later report that Stab, Panzer-Regiment 69 handed three command tanks to Panzer-Regiment 4 before leaving Italy. Given the dates I have assumed that this unit was organised under KstN 1103 dated 1 November 1943.

The fate of these Pzkpfw IV tanks is unknown but it is generally assumed that they were handed to one of the Pzkpfw IV-equipped battalions operating in Italy at the time. Three were reported as being fully serviceable in late February 1944.

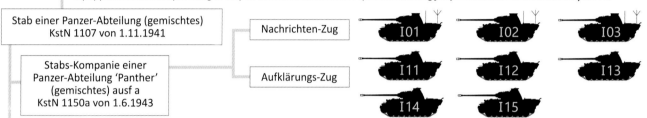

Although the 19 October 1943 order specified that the battalion headquarters was to be organised 'ohne Aufklärungs-Zug', or without its reconaissance platoon, the number of vehicles received and photographic evidence show that these five tanks were on hand and numbered as shown. The battalion headquarters was also allocated two Sdkfz 251/8 armoured ambulances and three Sdkfz 251/7 bridge-laying halftracks. The Panzer-Werkstatt-Zug 'Panther' operated two Bergepanther recovery vehicles which were both destroyed by their own crews in late June 1944. The Fliegerabwehr-Zug, or anti-aircraft platoon, was equipped with three Sdkfz 7/1 halftracks but they are not mentioned in any strength returns before March 1944.

Each of the battalion's Panzer companies was organised in accordance with mittlere Panzer-Kompanie 'Panther' (gemischtes) KstN 1177 von 10.1.1943 which authorised seventeen tanks instead of the twenty-two vehicles allocated to other Panther companies at this time.

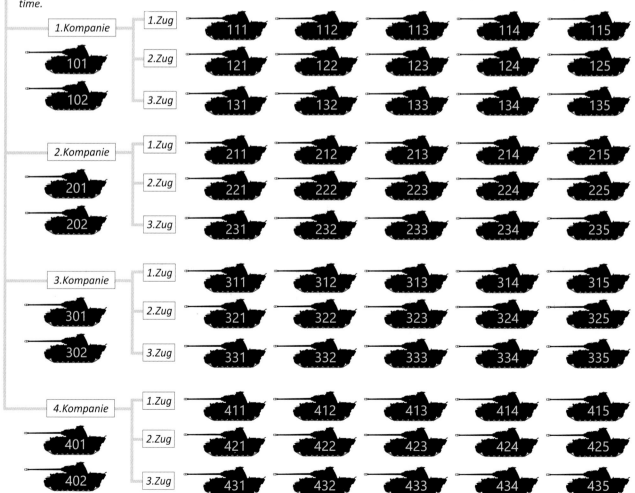

I.ABTEILUNG, PANZER-REGIMENT 4, OCTOBER 1944

In April 1944, Stab, Panzer-Regiment 69 left the battalion, handing over three Panzerbefehlswagen command tanks to I.Abteilung Panzer-Regiment 4, and eventually returned to Germany. By October 1944 the headquarters of I.Abteilung had been reduced to one Panzerbefehlswagen V command tank and one Panther and these were formed into a single platoon. The Fliegerabwehr-Zug retained its three Sdkfz 7/1 halftracks and the Pionier-Zug could field just one Sdkfz 251/7. No mention is made of the Sanitäts-Zug and its Sdkfz 251/8 armoured ambulances.

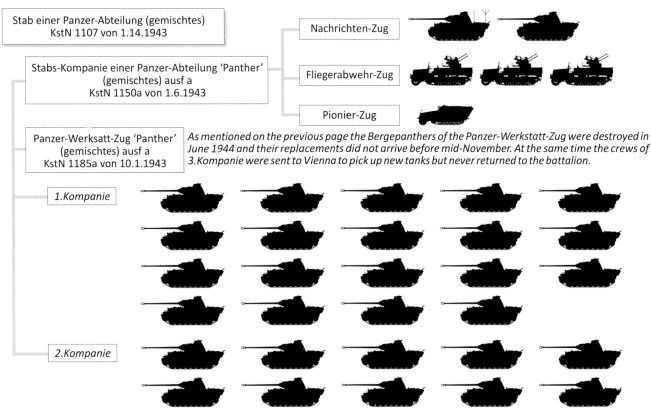

Stab einer Panzer-Abteilung (gemischtes)
KstN 1107 von 1.14.1943

Stabs-Kompanie einer Panzer-Abteilung 'Panther'
(gemischtes) ausf a
KstN 1150a von 1.6.1943

Nachrichten-Zug

Fliegerabwehr-Zug

Pionier-Zug

Panzer-Werksatt-Zug 'Panther'
(gemischtes) ausf a
KstN 1185a von 10.1.1943

As mentioned on the previous page the Bergepanthers of the Panzer-Werkstatt-Zug were destroyed in June 1944 and their replacements did not arrive before mid-November. At the same time the crews of 3.Kompanie were sent to Vienna to pick up new tanks but never returned to the battalion.

1.Kompanie

2.Kompanie

On 16 September 1944 the surviving five tanks of 4.Kompanie (401, 412, 413, 423 and 424) had been handed over to 2.Kompanie giving the total of ten shown here. At the same time twenty Panthers were shipped to the battalion and these all went to 1.Kompanie. On the last day of October a total of ten new Panthers were shipped from Heereszeugamt Breslau to Nachschub Italien and then on to the battalion and these were the last replacements to be received. Of the twenty-nine tanks on hand with 1.Kompanie and 2.Kompanie, eight were in short term-repair while seven were in long-term repair and could not be expected back in under three weeks.

I.ABTEILUNG, PANZER-REGIMENT 26, MARCH 1945

On 12 February 1945, I.Abteilung, Panzer-Regiment 4 was incorporated into 26.Panzer-Division as the first battalion of the division's Panzer regiment and renamed I.Abteilung, Panzer-Regiment 26. As mentioned above, 3.Kompanie had been sent to Vienna and from there eventually returned to Germany, never rejoining the battalion. Of the twenty-six tanks on hand a total of twenty-one were considered fully operational. On 2 February 1945 two Bergepanther recovery tanks were allocated to the battalion.

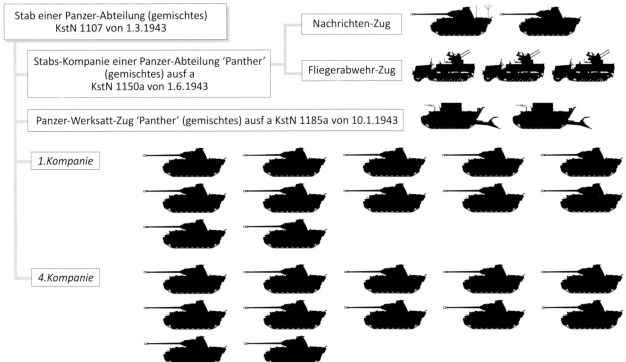

Stab einer Panzer-Abteilung (gemischtes)
KstN 1107 von 1.3.1943

Stabs-Kompanie einer Panzer-Abteilung 'Panther'
(gemischtes) ausf a
KstN 1150a von 1.6.1943

Nachrichten-Zug

Fliegerabwehr-Zug

Panzer-Werksatt-Zug 'Panther' (gemischtes) ausf a KstN 1185a von 10.1.1943

1.Kompanie

4.Kompanie

Dragon Models Ltd
B1-10/F., 603-609 Castle Peak Rd,
Kong Nam Industrial Building,
Tsuen Wan, N. T., Hong Kong
www.dragon-models.com

Tamiya Inc
Shizuoka City, Japan
www.tamiya.com

Trumpeter/Hobby Boss
NanLong Industrial Park, San Xiang,
ZhongShan, Guang Dong, China
www.trumpeter-china.com
www.hobbyboss.com

Academy Plastic Models
521-1, Yonghyeon-dong, Uijeongbu-si,
Gyeonggi-do, Korea
www.academy.co.kr

Hobby Fan/ AFV Club
6F ., No.183, Sec. 1, Datong Rd, Xizhi City,
Taipei County 221, Taiwan
www.hobbyfan.com

Royal Model
Via E. Montale, 19-95030 Pedara, Italy
www.royalmodel.com

Italeri S.p.A.
via Pradazzo 6/b,
40012 Calderara di Reno, Bologna, Italy
www.italeri.com

Takom
www.takom-world.com

Meng-Model
Galaxy Century Bldg., No. 3069 Caitian Rd,
Futian Dist., Shenzhen, Guangdong, China
www.meng-model.com

Amusing Hobby
3-16-19 Ima, Kita-ku, Okayama, Japan
www.amusinghobby.com

Rye Field Models
www.ryefield-model.com
An almost non-existent website. I would
recommend one of the on-line retailers.

Hauler
Jan Sobotka,
Moravská 38, 620 00 Brno,
Czech Republic
www.hauler.cz

Voyager
Room 501, No.411 4th Village,
SPC Jinshan District, Shanghai 200540,
China
www.voyagermodel.com

Griffon Model
Suite 501, Bldg 01, 418 Middle Longpan Rd,
Nanjing, China
www.griffonmodel.com

Aber
ul. Jalowcowa 15, 40-750 Katowice, Poland
www.aber.net.pl

E.T. Model
www.etmodeller.com

Friulmodel
H 8142. Urhida, Nefelejcs u. 2., Hungary
www.friulmodel.hu

Modelkasten
Chiyoda-ku Kanda, Nishiki-Cho 1-7, Tokyo,
Japan
www.modelkasten.com
Very difficult to navigate but worthwhile.

Airfix
www.airfix.com

Czech Master Kits (CMK)
Mezilesi 718/78,
19300 Praha 9,
Czech Republic
www.cmkkits.com

Eduard Model Accessories
Mirova 170, 435 21 Obrnice,
Czech Republic
www.eduard.com

Master Club
www.masterclub.ru
It appears that this firm is closely associated
with Armour35, a Russsian mail-order firm.

Model Artisan Mori
Yasutsugu Mori,
Maison Suiryu 302, Kunoshiro-cho 1-10,
Yokkaichi-City, Mie 510-0072, Japan
www.artisanmori.web.fc2.com

Tetra Model Works Co. Ltd.
2F, 18, Dorim-ro 126-gil, Yeongdeungpo-gu,
Seoul, 07299, Korea
www.tetramodel.com

RB Model
Powstancow Wlkp.29B,
64-360 Zbaszyn,
Poland
www.rbmodel.com

M Workshop Singapore
91 Bencoolen St, Sunshine Plaza 01-58,
Singapore
www.themworkshop.com

Zvezda (Zvezda-America)
www.zvezda-usa.com
Note that the Russian catalogue is not the
same as the US version.

ROCHM Model
www.rochmmodel.com
rochmmodel@gmail.com
This company has a huge selection of parts
and accessories for 1/35 scale Panther
models.

In writing this book I referred extensively to Germany's Panther Tank, The Quest for Combat Supremacy *written by the late Thomas L. Jentz with plan drawings by Hilary L. Doyle. Another invaluable resource was* Panther External Appearance & Design Changes *compiled by Roddy Macdougall and Martin Block. I would recommend Thomas Jentz's* Panzertruppen *books to any reader with an interest in German armour. Detailed coverage of German military units that served in the Italian campaign are rare and for the most part written in German, such as Ludwig Bauer's* Die Pantherabteilung Förster in Italien - Geschichte der I. Abteilung des Panzerregimentes 4 1943-1945. *Published in English is* Italienfeldzug: German Tanks and Vehicles 1943-1945 Vol.1 *and* Vol.2 *by Daniele Guglielmi and Mario Pieri and while these are impressive works they do not concentrate on the Panthers. I would like to thank the modellers who generously allowed me to publish the images of their work as well as Lisa Hooson and Stephen Chumbley, my editors at Pen & Sword. As always, I am indebted to Karl Berne, Valeri Polokov and J.Howard Parker for their invaluable assistance with the photographs and period insignia.*

Photographed in early February 1944, this Panther ausf A of 1.Kompanie, Panzer-Regiment 4 features the light mottled camouflage seen on many of the company's tanks. Note the roughly applied Zimmerit, indicative of tanks assembled by Daimler-Benz, 16-bolt reinforced road wheels and the early front fenders.